AUTOMOBILE
RECORD BREAKERS
FROM ROCKET TO ROAD CAR

AUTOMOBILE
RECORD BREAKERS

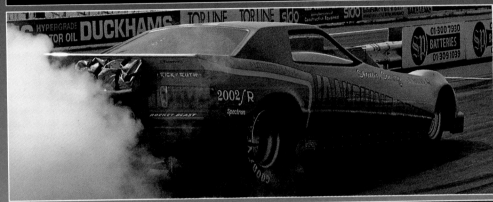

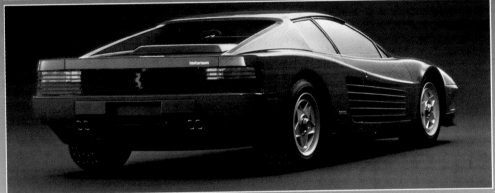

FROM ROCKET TO ROAD CAR

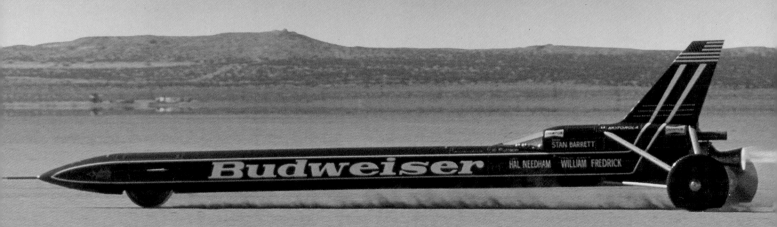

TIGER BOOKS INTERNATIONAL
LONDON

A QUINTET BOOK

This edition published in 1992 by
Tiger Books International plc, London

ISBN 1-85501-274-X

This book was designed and produced by
Quintet Publishing Limited
6 Blundell Street
London N7 9BH

Creative Director: Peter Bridgewater
Art Director: Ian Hunt
Designers: Stuart Walden, Beverley Miller
Editor: Shaun Barrington

Typeset in Great Britain by
Central Southern Typesetters, Eastbourne
Manufactured in Hong Kong by
Regent Publishing Services Limited
Printed in Hong Kong by
Leefung-Asco Printers Limited

CONTENTS

FOREWORD

Like many people, I have been waiting for this sort of book for a long time; in fact, since I first met David Tremayne in 1977 when I was lecturing on the Land Speed Record to any motor club who could spare the time to listen. From the start, it was clear he had a better LSR library than I, so books have been changing hands ever since.

He helped us considerably with the Land Speed Record programme in 1982–83, handling the public relations with the deft hand of a poacher turned gamekeeper and the confidence of a man who had simply learned as much as he possibly could on the subject.

All this was to pay off mightily for us when the official Project Thrust biographer, overloaded with records and data, failed to deliver, and David solemnly decided, regardless of the fact that the record was then a year old and market interest on the wane, that he was going to write his own book. The extraordinary thing about this was that once the decision had been made, the Thrust team heard nothing more until the manuscript miraculously appeared, and then members clubbed together to fund the initial print run. I was amazed by the book, since

it was so well written that it only needs the reading of a couple of pages today, some six years later, and one is transported right back into the midst of that struggle, when the only thing that mattered was The Record.

As we built up Project Thrust we learned a great deal about the media. The team joke was that there are two types of journalist – those who prefer to pontificate from the trackside, and those who want a ride. We usually got better results from those who took the risk and were strapped, controlless, into Thrust 2's second cockpit. Through our little mishap at Greenham in 1982 David missed his 260mph run in Thrust 2, but made up for it with a 250mph drive in Sammy Miller's Vanishing Point rocket car. Not so long ago he was riding at 80mph with champion Steve Curtis in a Class II offshore powerboat.

So here we have a fascinating book that brings together record, racing and road cars for the first time, written by one who combines the courage to have a go with a formidable talent for incisive and accurate reporting. I hope you enjoy it – I have, and I learned a lot.

RICHARD NOBLE

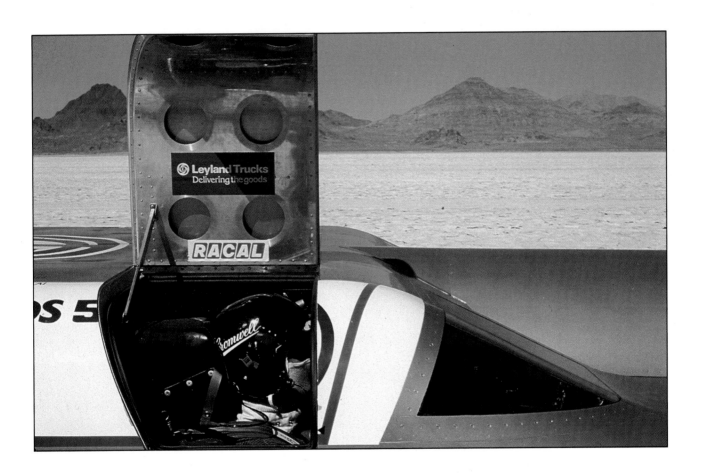

A man, a dream and a record. The desire to become the Fastest Man on Earth drove Richard Noble to Bonneville in 1981, where here he stares down the long black line prior to his 418mph run on October 10. Less than two years later, his speed an official 633,468mph, he had achieved his goal.

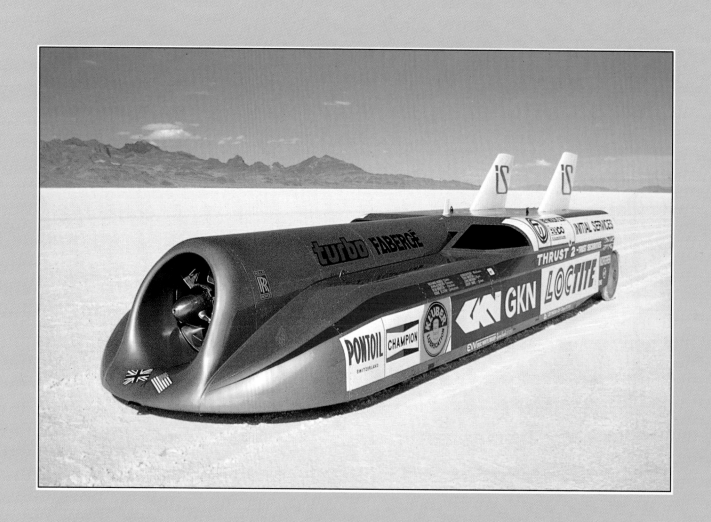

CHAPTER ONE

PROJECT THRUST

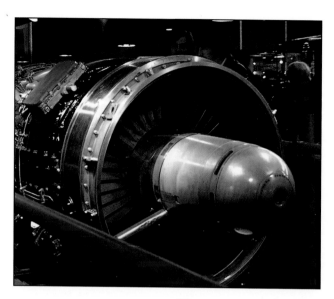

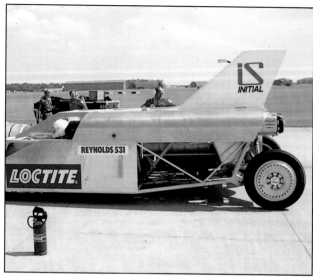

ABOVE LEFT *The starting point for Thrust 2 was this Rolls-Royce Avon 210 turbojet taken from a Lightning fighter plane. Having purchased it from the Ministry of Defence, Noble displayed it at the Earls Court Motorfair in October 1977 in a successful attempt to drum up financial and business support for his project.*

ABOVE RIGHT *Project Thrust proceeded as best it could, according to how much money Noble had been able to raise at any given point. By 1980 John Ackroyd had completed the design of the basic spaceframe chassis, and in this form, minus bodywork, it was run at airfields throughout Britain.*

The sight of a Lightning F2 accelerating vertically skywards, its twin afterburners belching plumes of flame, is awe-inspiring. It was one that Richard Noble, a 34-year-old businessman from Twickenham, England, had cause to ponder many times in 1980. Usually, if subconsciously, it would be as he sat strapped into a web of tubular steel poised for a take-off of his own.

Noble, was not, however, a fighter pilot. Instead, he was the driver and prime mover behind one of the most enterprising land speed record attempts ever launched. To his left in his spaceframe chassis nestled a single Lightning engine, a Rolls-Royce Avon 210 whose 15,000lb (635kg) of thrust was capable of propelling him to dizzying speeds.

Throughout the summer of that year, Noble got to know his peculiar creation as he undertook a series of test runs at airfields up and down the UK. As the driver of the beast he knew better than anyone that the only way to break the record, which stood then to the American Gary Gabelich at 622.407mph (1001.45kmh), was to approach it thoroughly and cautiously. His intimate research into its history had already convinced him that the days of the devil-may-care hot-rodder had long since passed.

Though he had little motorsport background, Noble was nonetheless an experienced jetcar driver when he first tried Thrust 2 at the Royal Air Force's Leconfield base at the end of July that year. Behind him lay the lessons — and the wreckage — of Thrust 1, Britain's first machine powered purely by the thrust of its exhaust gases. Knowing how expensive a record challenge would be, he had

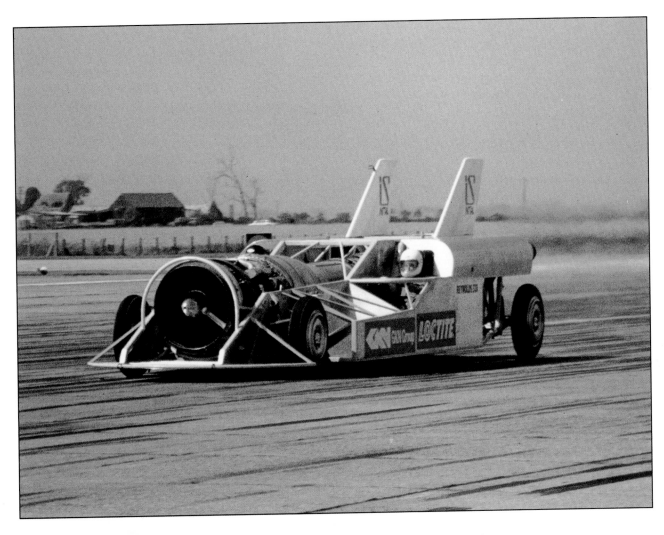

ABOVE *In his initial acclimatization runs at RAF Leconfield, Noble was troubled by traffic signs on the runway, and its bumpy state. A move to RAF Alconbury proved more satisfactory, and by the end of the summer of 1980 he had regularly exceeded 200mph while exciting thousands of spectators.*

set out with that car to prove that he had the determination and courage necessary for the task, and to establish the credibility that was vital if he was to attract financial support from a British economy then still in the throes of depression.

With a degree of cunning that was to characterise his campaign, he managed to beat the French air force to the last serviceable Rolls-Royce Derwent 8 jet engine left in Britain, purchasing it from a surplus yard in 1974 on the very day a French government inspector was due to examine it. It cost him a mere £200.

At the time he worked for the giant GKN automotive parts supplier, and a prowl round its experimental workshop revealed a ladder chassis which would be ideal for his purpose. With the persuasion that was also to be a crucial asset throughout the life of Project Thrust, he cajoled the manager not only into providing it free, but also into shortening it first!

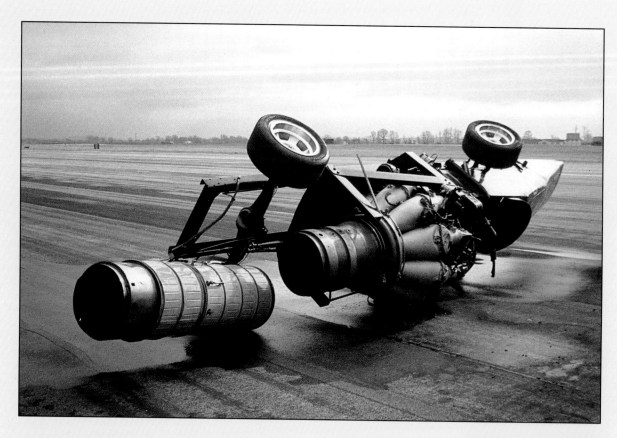

HIGH-SPEED LESSONS

Thrust 1 was a desperately crude machine, little more than a jet engine mounted on Wolfrace alloy wheels and racing slick tyres. Richard Noble called it a 'cathedral on wheels', but it taught him the rudiments of high-speed driving. It also taught him a lesson he would never forget. At the UK's RAF Fairford on 5 March, 1977 he undertook a series of fast test runs which ended disastrously as a wheel bearing seized at 140mph (225kmh). Thrust 1 was thrown into a horrifying series of rolls, turning over in mid-air with each lurch. When it finally came to

rest Noble was completely unhurt and stepped calmly out after releasing his safety harness. He was more satisfied that he had had the presence of mind to switch off the fuel supply in mid-air than he was concerned about the loss of his car. And that very night he began to plan Thrust 2. Already the signs of record-breaking credibility were emerging . . .

That incident was not the only time he would become a passenger in an out-of-control jetcar. On 16 June, 1982, just before departure for Bonneville, he put Thrust 2 through its final trials at Greenham Common, England.

Braking parachute specialist Mike Barrett was the passenger when Noble kept the power on a fraction too late: a small mistake which would blossom terrifyingly into a nightmare ride. The low-speed parachute streamed out as he pressed its eject button, but failed to open. Thrust 2 was simply going too fast.

At 180mph (289kmh) Noble slammed on the massive disc brakes and slid with his wheels locked and the tyres pluming smoke for 4000ft before arcing off the fast disappearing runway and across a rough grass verge in a series of frightening hops.

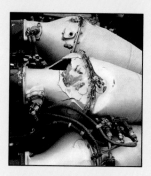

The aircraft tyres were worn right through to the canvas and dirt was thrown into the engine, but Thrust 2 stayed the right way up and Noble and Barrett escaped totally unharmed. The damage, estimated at £22,000, was repaired in time for the delayed 1982 attempt.

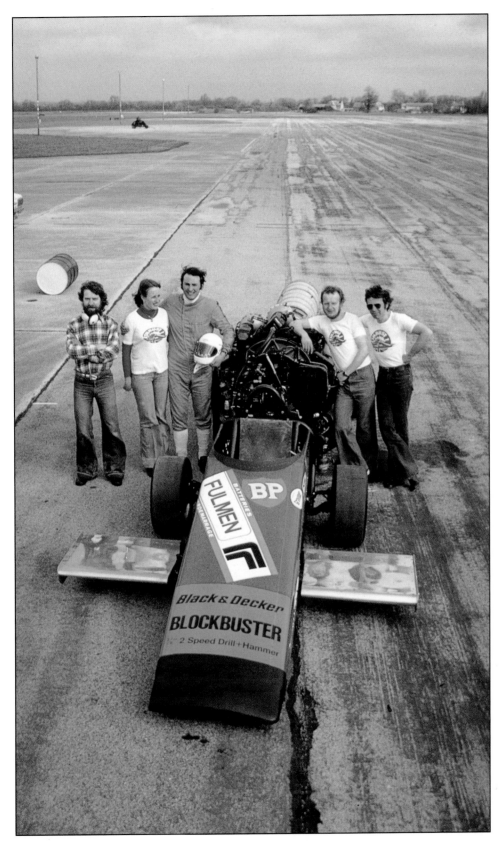

LEFT Noble took his first steps towards the Land Speed Record by designing and building Thrust 1, Britain's first-ever pure-thrust jetcar. He admits he made a lot of mistakes in its concept, and described it as a 'cathedral on wheels', but it provided him with invaluable experience.

OPPOSITE, TOP At RAF Fairfield on March 5 1977, shortly after the photo on the immediate left was taken, he received his first lesson in high-speed car control. When a wheel bearing seized at 140mph, Thrust 1 was thrown into a series of airborne rolls, from which he was lucky to escape totally unharmed.

OPPOSITE, BOTTOM Thrust 1 was less fortunate. The car was wrecked, and so was the precious Rolls-Royce Derwent 8 jet engine. Noble had purchased it for a mere £200, which was a pittance for its useful 3,500 lbs of thrust.

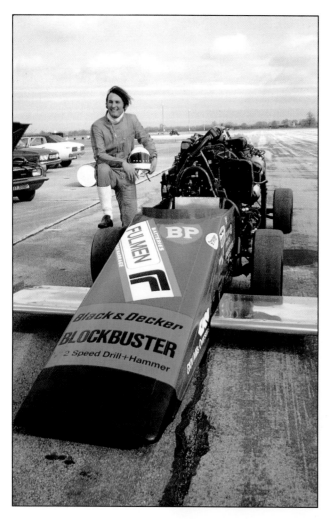

THRUST 2

Thrust 1 proved a useful publicity tool, but was eventually destroyed in a high-speed roll in 1977. After Noble towed the wreckage to a scrap dealer immediately afterwards, he and his small team held an emergency meeting. They had three alternatives: they could give up; they could build another version of the car; or they could move on to something new. Predictably, Noble took the final option. Thrust 2 would be bigger, more powerful and, above all, faster. It would be fast enough to attract the money to build Thrust 3, which would be the land speed record car.

Within months of the Thrust 1 accident, Noble addressed a meeting of senior RAF directors, who were keen to help. They were more than a little surprised when he asked them outright for a complete scrap Lightning fighter plane, but though they couldn't meet that request, his outrageous approach eventually yielded the Avon engine. What had originally cost the British government thousands of pounds swapped hands for only £500, and when he showed the Avon at the Earl's Court Motorfair that October, Project Thrust was back on the road.

When Thrust 2 finally appeared in 1980 it was far from finished. What thousands saw at air shows throughout Britain was merely the skeleton, the spaceframe chassis designed by John Ackroyd and its massive jet engine which occupied its entire 27ft (8.23m) length. The driver sat to its right, while the left-hand side contained a

ABOVE *Even at this early stage of his record breaking career in 1977, Noble displayed a remarkable ability to attract sponsors to his unusual venture.*

RIGHT *From the outset, giving his financial supporters a clear idea of the undertaking was a cornerstone of his management style. Involving sponsors in this close manner would remain an unusual characteristic throughout Project Thrust's life.*

OPPOSITE, LEFT *The Rolls-Royce Derwent 8 jet engine was the last available in Britain.*

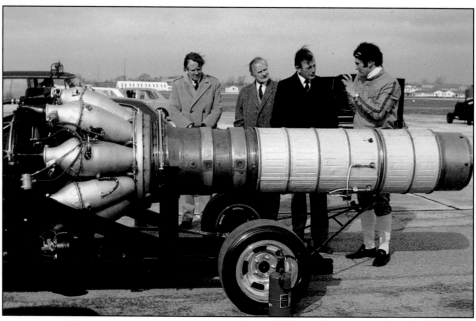

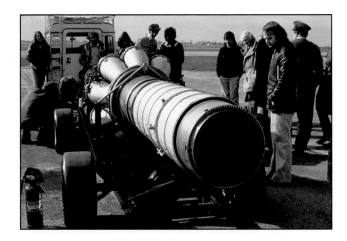

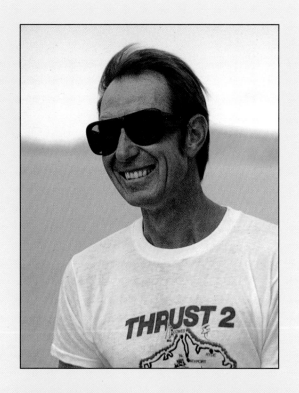

seat for intrepid passengers! It wasn't simply there to balance the aesthetics, either: the shrewd Noble saw it as a perfect means of giving potential sponsors a frightening insight into the challenge he faced.

By September he was ready for the first hurdle, the British land speed record. The outright figure had last been set in the country when Sir Malcolm Campbell managed 174.88mph (281.15kmh) at Wales' Pendine Sands in 1927, but as it soared beyond 600mph (965.4kmh) on American salt in the intervening years, British clothing magnate Richard Horne had pushed the British mark to 191.64mph (308.34kmh) in his racing Ferrari 512 sports car.

Noble chose the Greenham Common, England RAF base because it had the longest runway available. Pendine would have been totally unsuitable for a four-ton monster, even if Ministry of Defence property had not rendered parts of it unavailable. Thrust 2 required a flat, smooth surface, and Greenham's 10,000ft (3050m) was just sufficient. Noble knew he couldn't afford the slightest mistake in such a confined course, but proved equal to his task with a series of new records. 248.87mph (400.43kmh) for two passes through the measured mile gained him the new British record.

By 1981 he had raised the final amounts of sponsorship and pushed the project ahead. From an ugly duckling Thrust 2 grew into a sleek aluminium-skinned projectile that fitted perfectly into the lunarscape surroundings when it arrived at the legendary Bonneville Salt Flats in late September.

Within some members of the team, building the giant car had created an almost unshakeable belief in its superiority. It didn't take long, however, before teething problems began to sap their morale.

JOHN ACKROYD

John Ackroyd was sitting on a beach reading a copy of *Cars & Car Conversions* magazine when he first learned of Richard Noble's plans to break the land speed record. In fact, what he read was an ingenious advertisement that Noble had placed, seeking a designer for a 650mph (1046kmh) car! Bluebird designer Ken Norris had agreed to vet applicants for the job, but when Noble called Ken to tell him to expect a visitor called Ackroyd, John was already there, awaiting interview. That was the sort of enthusiasm that had taken him through jobs with ERA and aircraft companies such as Britten-Norman and Dornier, and saw him mastermind the design and manufacture of the Enfield 8000 electric car. Norris recommended him immediately, and while Noble went off to find the money to employ him, John took a temporary design job at Porsche. He was being headhunted by Messerschmidt when the call finally came to join Project Thrust.

He took Noble's basic design concept, with the 27ft (8m) Rolls-Royce Avon engine slung centrally in a spaceframe chassis with cockpits either side, and refined it into a car that required minimal significant changes throughout its life. An adventurer like Noble, he rode as his passenger at speeds up to 400mph (743kmh) during the initial stability problems.

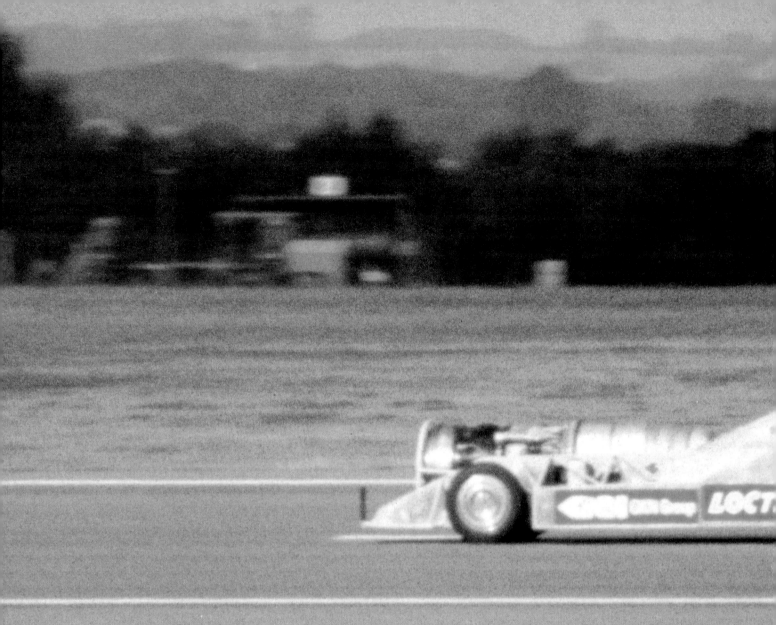

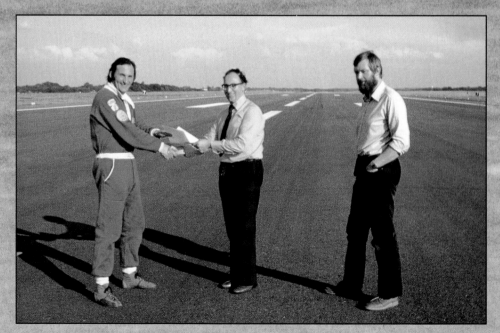

RIGHT *After his Flying Mile run, which gave him the British Land Speed Record, Noble receives the official confirmation from the RAC timekeepers. It was another milestone in Project Thrust's development.*

MAIN PICTURE AND INSET, OPPOSITE *At RAF Greenham Common on 24th and 25th September 1980, Noble drove Thrust 2 to a series of national records, ranging from 149.57mph for the standing start kilometre and 166.47mph for the standing start mile, to 248.87mph for the Flying Mile.*

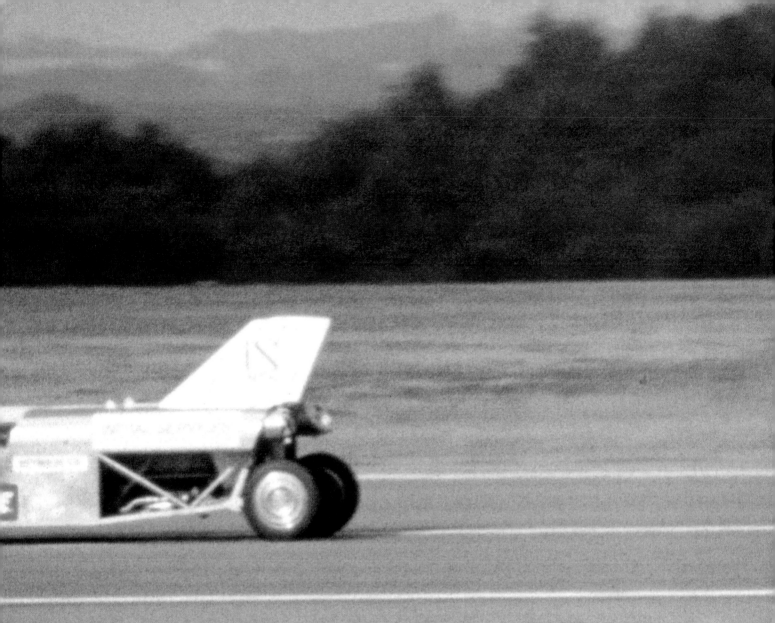

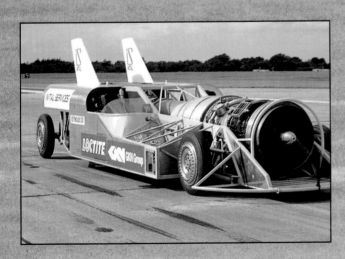

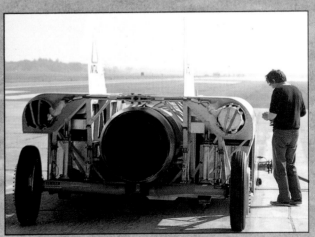

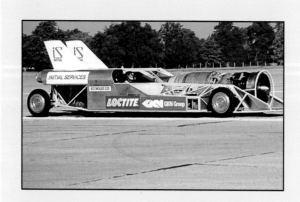

THRUST 2's ANATOMY

Art Arfons' Green Monster was the first car to use the format of a cockpit either side of a centrally-mounted jet engine, but Ackroyd's execution of Thrust 2 was brilliant in its simplicity and engineering integrity. 27ft long, 8ft wide, it weight four tons and comprised an aluminium skin rivetted to a steel spaceframe chassis. Ackroyd also designed the spun aluminium wheels, which had small keels upon which the car would rise and plane across the salt or desert surface at speeds over 250mph (402kmh).

When he first approached British Aerospace, which conducted the initial wind tunnel tests, its technicians were openly sceptical about the effectiveness of Thrust 2's boxy shape, but it had been very cleverly conceived. The tests themselves revealed not only that Ackroyd had done his sums exceptionally well, but that Thrust 2, initially intended as a showcase for the record-attempting

Thrust 3, had itself sufficient potential to establish a new mark. Its chances of doing that were further enhanced when the Rolls-Royce Avon 210 engine, with 15,000lb (817kg) of thrust, was exchanged for a 302 with 17,500lb (7945kg) before the Bonneville attempt in 1981. Braking was via large disc brakes specially conceived by Lucas-Girling, but they were only used below 200mph (322kmh). Above that speed a system of parachutes was used. In its brief active life Thrust 2 set six national and four international records.

TOP AND RIGHT *The Rolls-Royce Avon 210 turbojet dominated Thrust 2, with the driver's cockpit to the right of it and another, for intrepid passengers, to the left. The twin tail fins helped prevent yaw at speed, and exerted less lifting force than would a single, taller fin.*

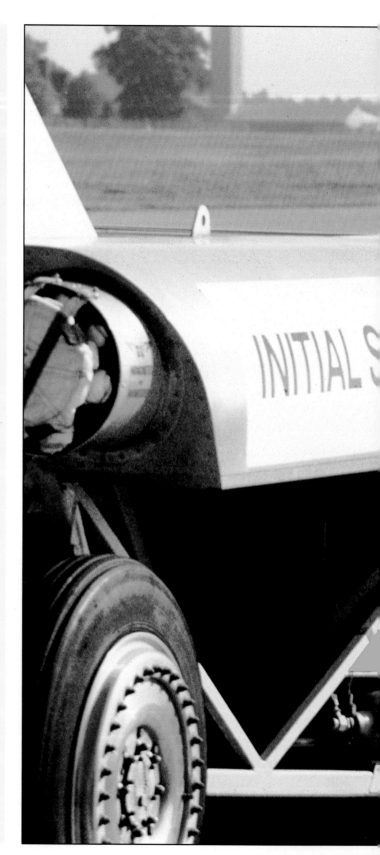

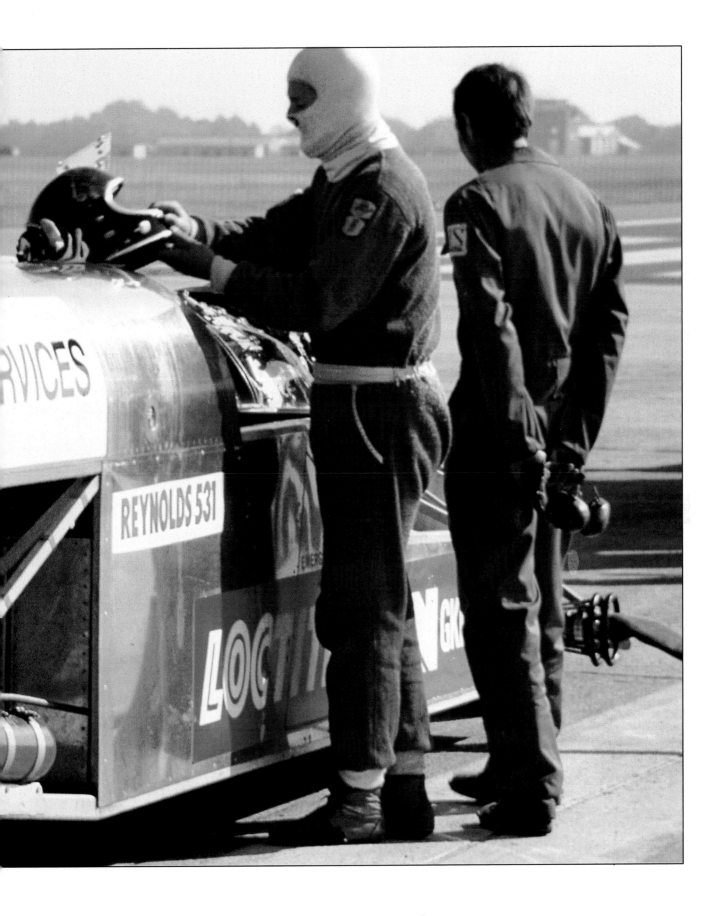

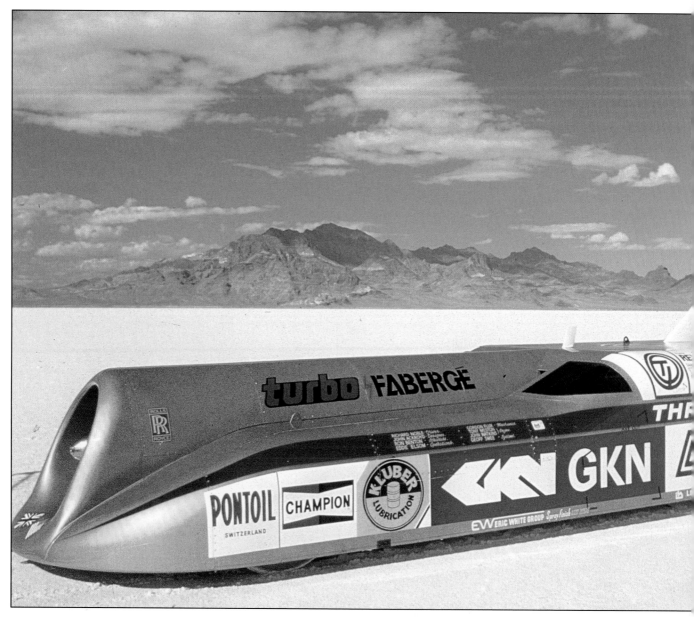

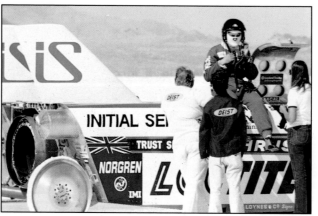

LEFT *Noble prepares his first run on the salt, aided (left to right) by Jim Deist and his nephew Butch, and wife Sally. Safety equipment manufacturer Deist was instrumental in introducing the parachute as a high-speed brake for land speed cars, and he and Butch had been present at most attempts since the Sixties.*

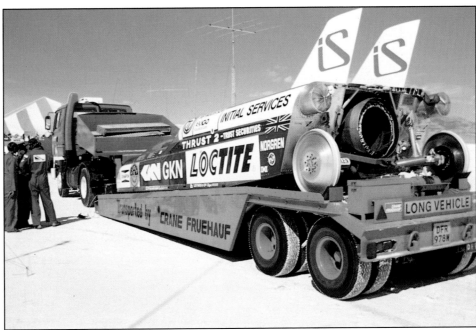

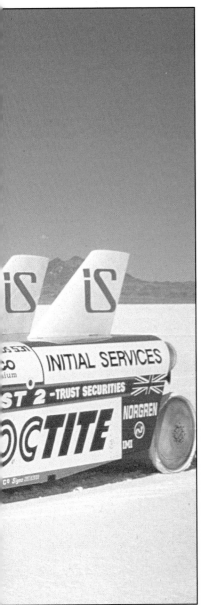

Although Thrust 2 had used Dunlop tyres on aircraft wheels during its British airfield tests, it had always been designed to run on solid aluminium wheels once it reached the salt. As soon as Noble reached speeds of 300mph (482.7kmh) on them he found the car very difficult to control. Although on the face of it all he had to do was put his foot down and steer it, record-breaking is far more complicated. Before he could aim for 600mph (965.4kmh), he had to ease up the speed in planned increments as his technicians monitored each new step. At this stage an American might have gone faster, because the Americans had been running pure thrust cars for years. The British, however, had no experience of such cars and had to proceed with caution.

To begin with, each time Noble went over 300 (482.7) Thrust 2 began to veer from its special course which had been painstakingly scraped flat. Many times he simply became a passenger as it slithered alarmingly into the rougher salt. Compounding the stability problem, the salt itself was too soft and the metal wheels cut deep ruts in the specially prepared 'lanes'. Noble had to make a run in each direction under the rules governing record breaking, and described hitting first-run furrows on his return as like hitting London's Clapham Junction railway lines at 250mph!

The team, disillusioned as its troubles mounted, struggled on. Designer Ackroyd tried linking the independent rear suspension arms to make a solid rear axle, without

ABOVE *The problem of transporting a four ton car that was 27 feet long and eight wide was solved with this special Crane Fruehauf trailer. It was towed by a Leyland T45 Roadtrain cab. Subsequent monitoring of Thrust 2's behaviour at 600mph indicated it actually had a rougher ride on its trailer while being transported to the record venue.*

ABOVE LEFT *The dream comes true. Thrust 2 poses on the hallowed salt of Bonneville in September 1981, shortly after the team arrived. By this time it was cloaked in its sleek aluminium shell, which bears ample testimony to Noble's ability to attract commercial backing.*

noticeable improvement, but minor changes to the front suspension toe-in settings had a major beneficial effect. With stability dramatically enhanced, Noble achieved 392.720mph (892.72kmh) on October 10. A long way from the record, but it was progress. And the return run brought a major breakthrough.

While stability problems continued, he had used only the basic power of the Avon turbojet. The reheat or 'after-burner' in a jet engine is a device that injects neat fuel into the flow of gases in the tailpipe to ignite unburnt oxygen and increase thrust significantly. Noble, however, believed that using the reheat would make the stability problems worse, but Thrust had behaved much better on his first run, and on his return he used it for the first time. The effect was electrifying.

Spurting its distinctive deep orange flame, Thrust 2 stormed through the timing traps at 447.029mph (719.269kmh), its best speed yet. The average of the two runs gave Noble a speed of 418.118mph (672.751kmh), which made him the fastest Briton in history.

That night, as the car was prepared for faster runs the following day, the poor weather that had dogged the team on and off since its arrival returned. By the morning Bonneville had literally been transformed into a lake. There was no option but to call a halt to the attempt.

Project Thrust returned to Britain and Noble immediately began preparing for another go in 1982. Ackroyd incorporated some minor changes, the most significant of which were a new fuel system and 6in (15.24cm) wide front wheels instead of the previous 4in (10.1cm) ones to improve stability further. By June everything was ready, and the weather reports from Bonneville sounded favourable. That month Thrust 2 returned to Greenham Common, not for more British record attempts but purely for a final check. This time, however, Noble made a minor driving error that severely damaged the car and delayed the project for another three months.

BLACK ROCK

By the time Thrust 2 was ready again for Bonneville it was September. Normally that would have presented little problem. After all, Gabelich had set his record in the rocket-propelled Blue Flame in October. This time, however, came yet another of those setbacks that ensure nothing ever comes easily in record-breaking. By the time Thrust 2 had arrived in Utah, the salt flats were under so

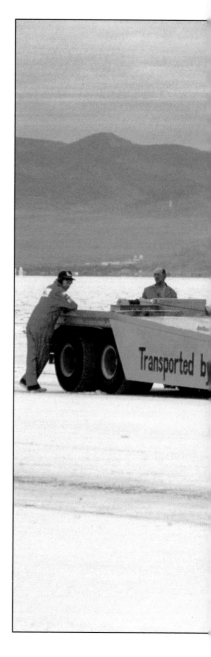

ABOVE *Once the Leyland T45 Roadtrain cab had been detached, Thrust 2 was winched nose-first off the Fruehauf trailer. Offloading called for care and precision to avoid damaging the projectile's underside.*

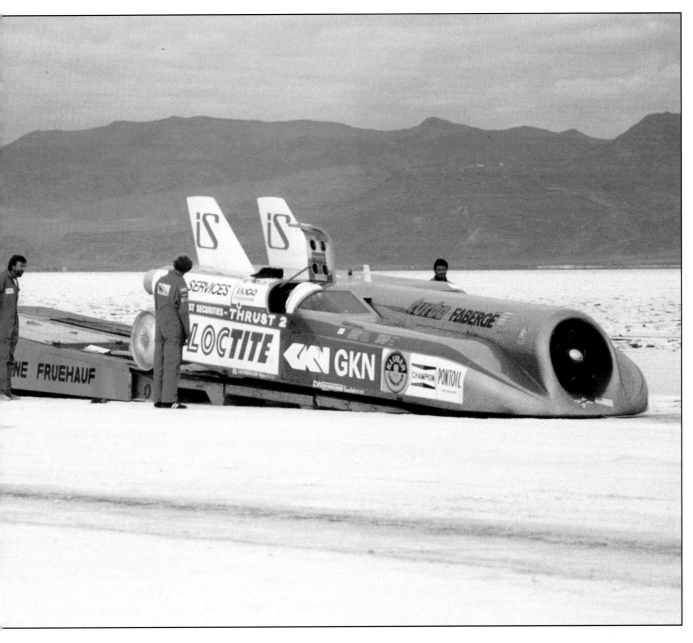

much water that Noble and Ackroyd actually swam their intended course!

The previous year they had at least achieved a peak speed close to 500mph (804kmh). This time, it seemed, the giant jetcar wasn't even going to turn a wheel in anger. But Noble couldn't give up as his already limited budget was shrinking and, within days, he had found an alternative. In a week the entire team had been transported across-state to Nevada, 120 miles north of gambling town Reno, to the dusty Black Rock Desert.

There, as winter edged round the project, Noble and

Thrust 2 resumed where they had left off the previous year and worked steadily closer to Gabelich's speed. The 500mph (804kmh) barrier was broken, then 550mph (885kmh). Then 575mph (920kmh). The cracks in the fledgling team's organization were becoming more exposed as the speeds rose, but after a successful fight against environmentalists who objected to the desert being used for such purposes, morale remained high. Where occasional poor weather brought the odd grumble of discontent at times, as the tedium of waiting got the better of some, higher speeds swept away any bad feel-

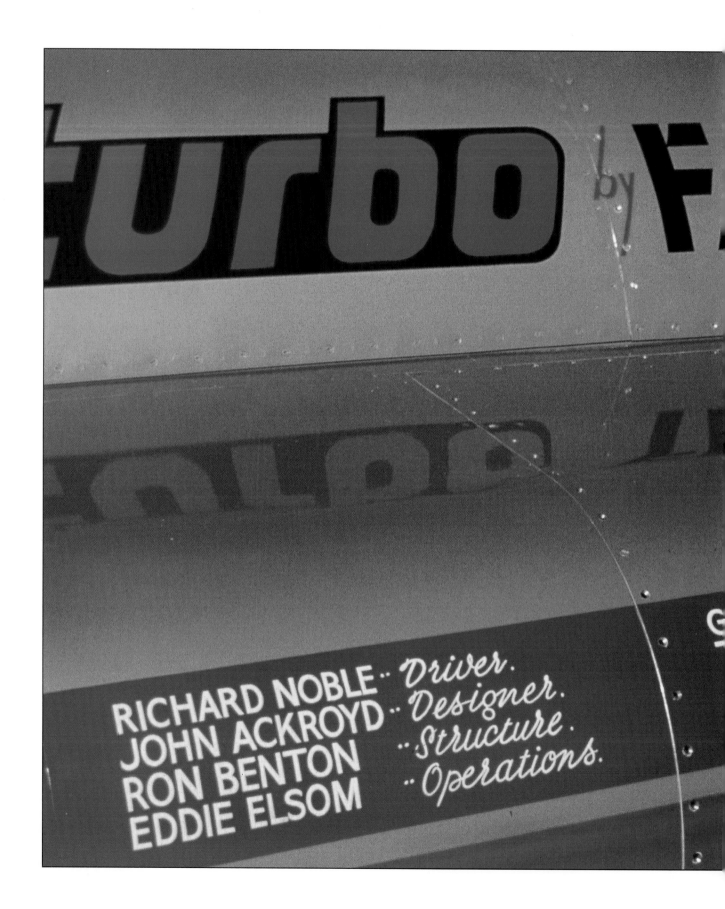

LEFT *No land speed record has ever been won without solid teamwork, and Noble was keen that the efforts of his principal crew members should be recognised on Thurst 2. This was part of the line-up in 1981, but by 1983 Geoff Smee's place had been taken by Gordon Biles, and that year George Webb was also instrumental in helping John Watkins when engine problems arose.*

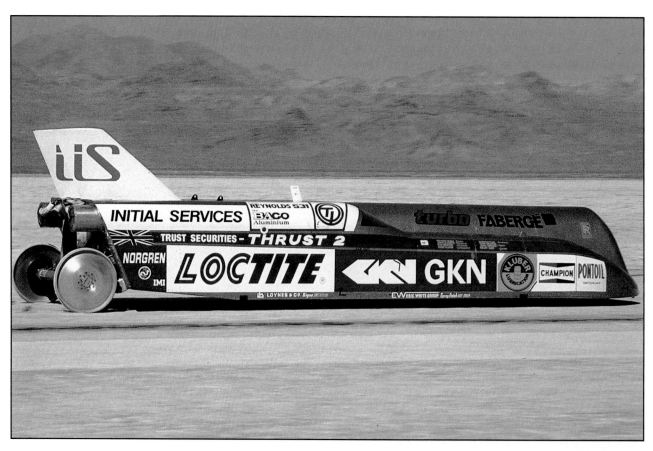

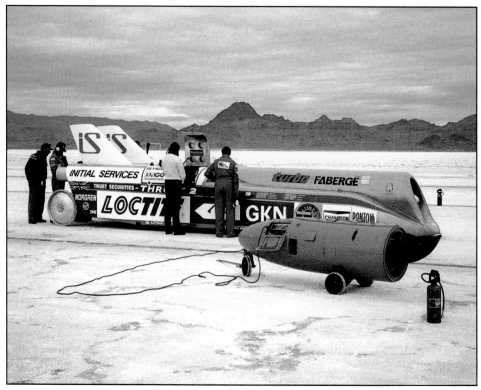

ABOVE *Against the backdrop of the famous Silver Island Mountains, Noble accelerates Thrust 2 at the start of a run. Motion was always deceptive. At first it moved slowly, then blasted on to the horizon as the jet's power was unleashed. Watched from a distance, however, the car would again seem sluggish, even when travelling beyond 600mph. Such was the mirage effect, it frequently seemed to be riding on water.*

RIGHT *The orange bullet-shaped object in the foreground is one of the small Palouste gas turbine engines which were used to start Thrust 2's Avon. The smaller unit was connected to the larger by flexible trunking.*

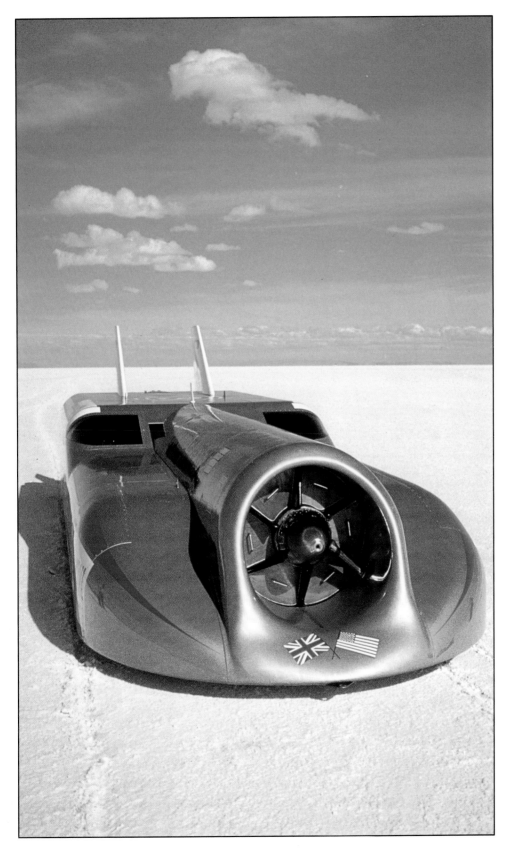

LEFT *Alone on the salt in perfect weather conditions, Thrust 2 always looked in its element. The twin cockpits and tail fins are clearly illustrated in this shot, which also captures something of the tremendous isolation of the vast salt flats. The wooden panels in the engine intake protected it from debris when the car was 'off-duty'.*

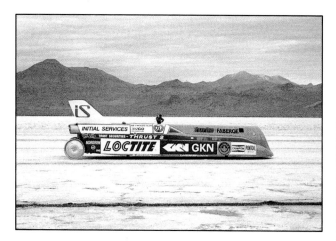

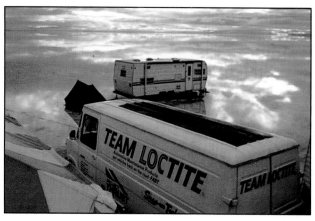

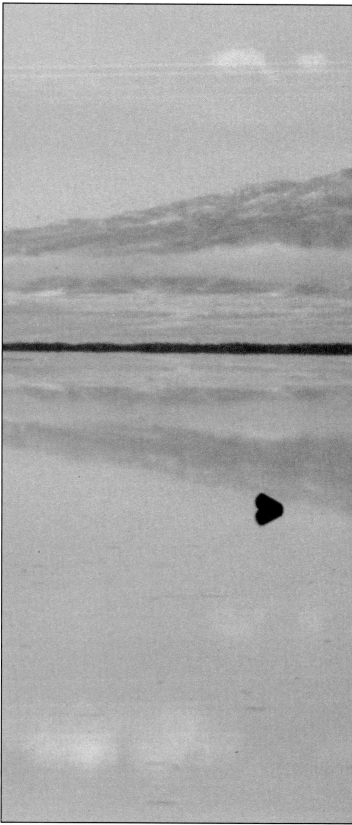

ing. By November Noble was taking aim at 600mph (965kmh).

Ultimately, he failed. Thrust reached an average of 590.551mph (950.196kmh) on the 4th, but the engine didn't seem to have enough power, the course was shorter than intended because one end remained wet, and the reheat refused to operate properly. Worse, the weather was deteriorating again. This time Noble had taken his car to the very edge of success, only to be driven away again without the record. He would be able to muster the financial resources for another try in 1983, but he knew it would be the last time.

That year Thrust 2 was completely rebuilt. Rolls-Royce finally agreed to boost the engine, having steadfastly refused to become officially involved in previous years. Now the Avon 302 really did have its full 17,500lb (7945kg) of thrust, and Ackroyd again incorporated minor but important changes. The underfloor was smoother to reduce drag, the fuel system was revised again, and small additional coil springs were fitted to aid the innovative rubber springs he had specified from the start.

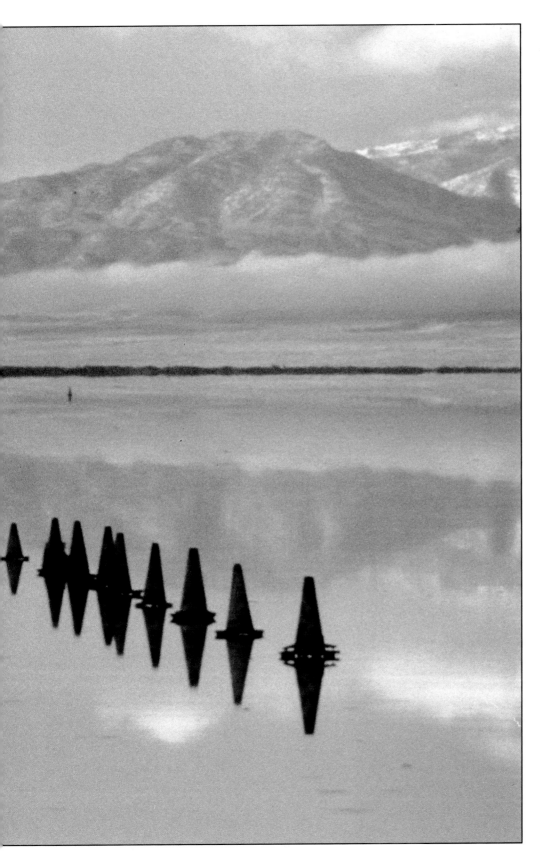

FAR LEFT, ABOVE *The ragged nature of the salt results from brine beneath it being drawn to the surface by the sun and then evaporating, so that the hard deposits leave little pressure ridges. Noble's crew had to scrape the entire 11-mile surface of its intended track with a heavy truck-drawn drag to make it as smooth as possible, and each 'lane' was then defined with a black line.*

FAR LEFT, BELOW *All the painstaking work was literally washed out when the rains came in early October 1981.*

LEFT *As far as the eye could see, the thousand-square-mileage of Bonneville was beneath water within hours of Noble achieving his 418,118mph average on October 10 1981, and any further runs were clearly out of the question.*

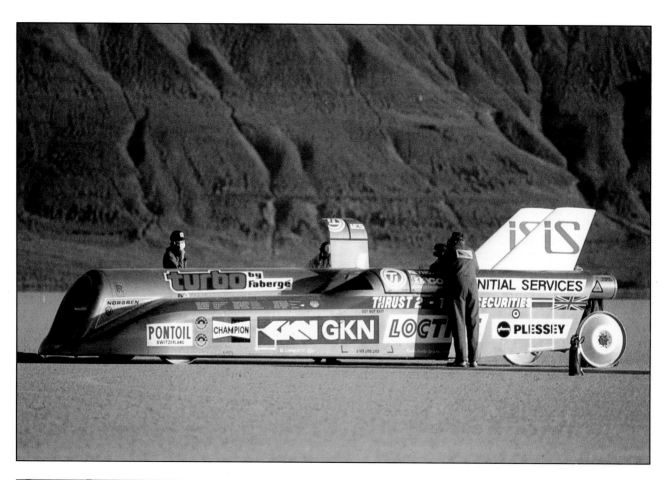

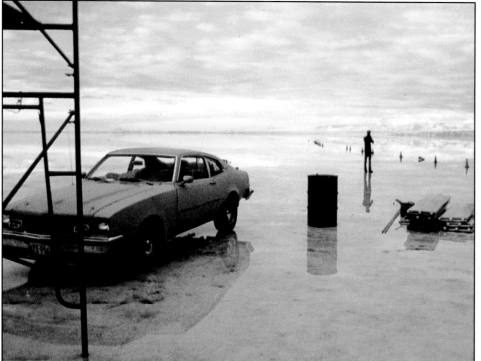

ABOVE RIGHT *Black Rock Desert was in many ways a much happier place for Project Thrust, whose crew members immediately integrated with the friendly locals. As Noble moved closer to the record in 1983, his activities always attracted a crowd, even though the hamlet of Gerlach was 120 miles from Reno.*

LEFT *The new venue helped to erase memories of the 1981 flood which not only wrecked the base camp, but washed away much of the fledgling team's morale.*

ABOVE *Within days of Bonneville flooding for the second successive year, in 1982, Project Thrust relocated to the Black Rock Desert.*

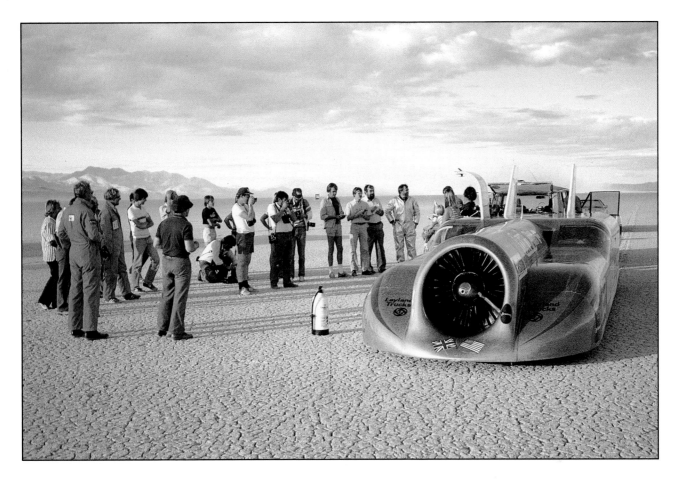

By September the team was back in America. Bonneville was still unsuitable, but Ackroyd's most significant data had in any case been accrued at Black Rock, and that location was the logical choice once again. By then, the team had been strengthened by the presence of Bluebird designer Ken Norris as manager, and the whole outfit had a much more professional air. Again, however, the road would be rocky.

The initial runs proved that the car accelerated faster than ever. Noble averaged 394.477mph (634,713kmh) in a mere three-quarters of a mile (1.2km), and reached a peak of 460mph (740kmh) in only 27 seconds. With 11 miles (17.6km) of flat desert at his disposal, the chances of a record at last seemed good.

Then the problems began. On his fourth run of the new attempt, he couldn't get the reheat to work properly, but on the fifth he officially averaged over 600mph (965.4kmh) for the first time with 608.416 (975.723) through the mile. Record attempts may be measured over either a kilometre or a mile, but where both distances yield new records the governing body, FISA in Paris, pre-

fers the mile since it is longer. If Noble could average better than 606.6 (976.0) on his return run he would break Craig Breedlove's 600.601mph (966.367kmh) jet-car record.

Instead, although he managed 606.4 (975.6) and broke that mark by 6mph (9.6kmh), he didn't do so by the required margin of one per cent. At the time it didn't seem a problem, but it was the first sign of trouble, for Thrust 2's peak speeds were proving very little higher than its averages, an indication that it had ceased to accelerate. The worry set in that perhaps, after all, 17,500lb (7945kg) of thrust simply wasn't enough.

DRAG AND SURGE

Thrust 2 was now moving at speeds bettered only by Gabelich's totally dissimilar rocket car, and as well as the power problem Ackroyd began to worry about the effects of drag. Although Thrust 2 wasn't travelling anywhere near the speed of sound, airflow over its cockpit screens and wheel covers *was*, and the effects of transonic drag

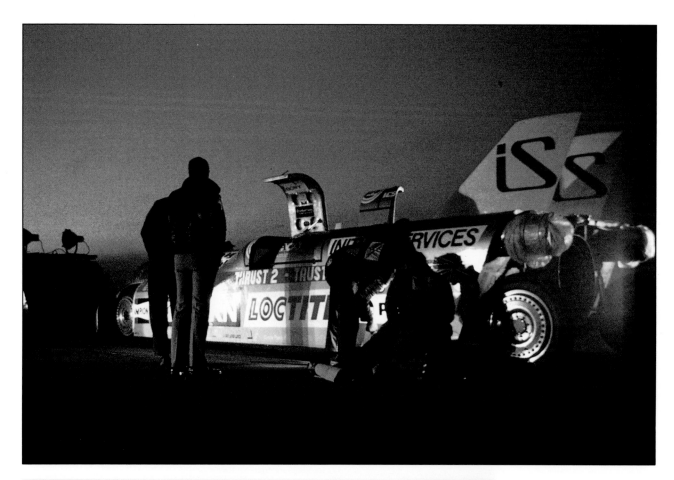

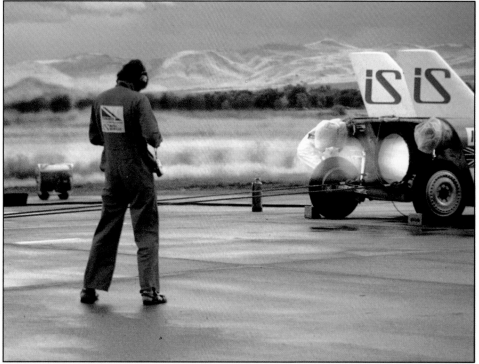

ABOVE *When it was suspected in 1982 that the Avon engine wasn't giving its full power, Operations Director Eddie Elsom called the Base Commander at nearby Fallon to ask if Project Thrust could use his facilities to conduct a static engine test. No sooner had he agreed and put the phone down, than the team drove in the gates . . .*

LEFT *In 1983 another static test was essential after the fears that the Avon had been damaged by overheating. At Reno Airport the team's parachute expert Mike Barrett (Noble's passenger during the 1982 accident at Greenham Common) watches the reheat's 'dancing diamonds' which indicated a healthy powerplant.*

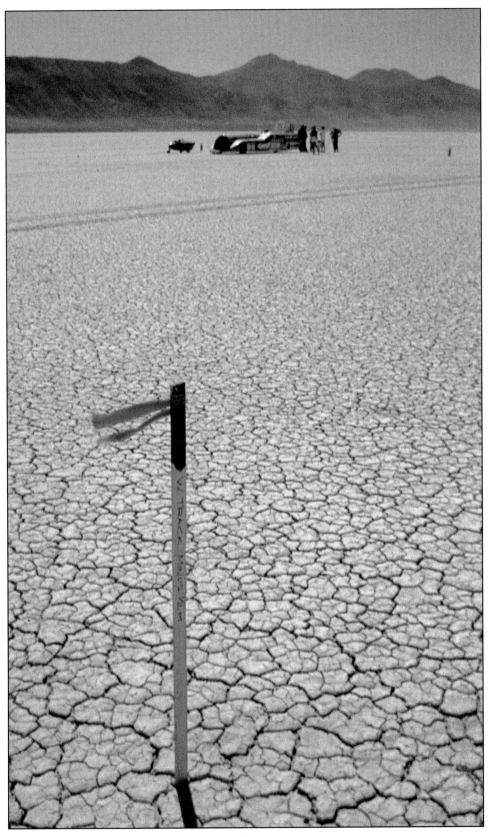

LEFT *A bad sign. Whenever the wind sidled above 5mph, USAC's officials were reluctant to let Thrust 2 run. This was one of many such delays in 1983. The wind sock's stake is driven into the playa's interesting polygonal surface, which differed significantly from Bonneville's crunchy but potentially very hard salt make-up.*

BELOW *Thrust 2's 30-inch wheels also acted as its tyres. They were cast in aluminium, weighed about 100 lbs each, and had specially bead-blasted rims to provide grip. The rear wheels had special keels on which the car planed above 250mph. At maximum speed they rotated at 8,000rpm, or 705mph.*

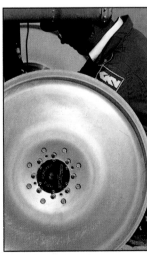

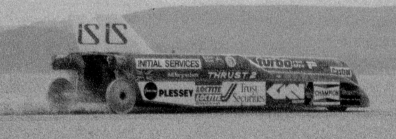

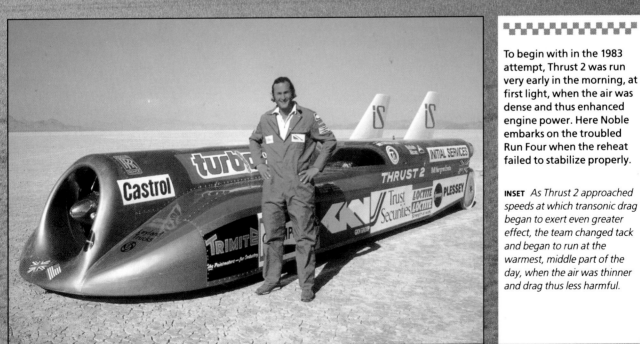

To begin with in the 1983 attempt, Thrust 2 was run very early in the morning, at first light, when the air was dense and thus enhanced engine power. Here Noble embarks on the troubled Run Four when the reheat failed to stabilize properly.

INSET *As Thrust 2 approached speeds at which transonic drag began to exert even greater effect, the team changed tack and began to run at the warmest, middle part of the day, when the air was thinner and drag thus less harmful.*

RIGHT *Long before it ever embarked on a run, Thrust 2 was thoroughly checked. Noble prepares to run through his external checks as Barrett loads the day's parachute launching mortars. To the left is the flexible trunking connecting the Palouste to the Avon.*

OPPOSITE *Bluebird designer and Thrust team manager Ken Norris discusses parachutes with Ackroyd (white hat) and Barrett, as chief engineer Gordon Flux checks the engine intake and John Norris loads the film camera in the passenger cockpit.*

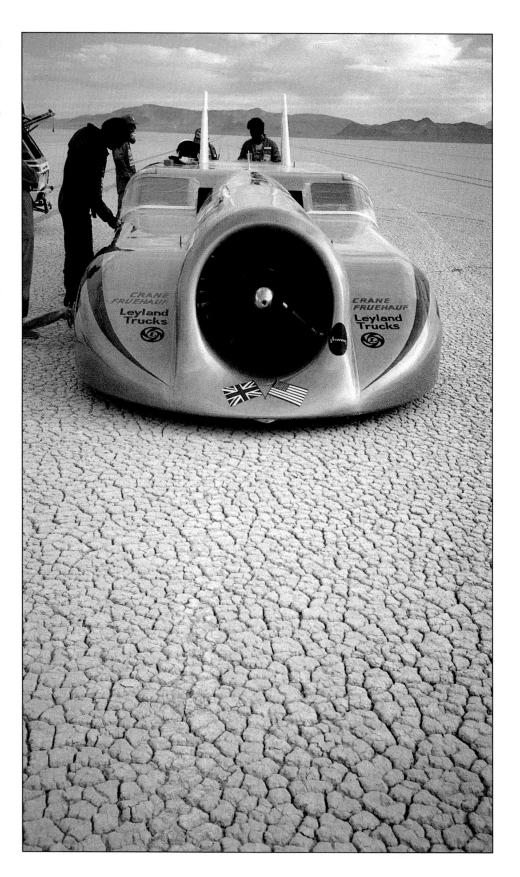

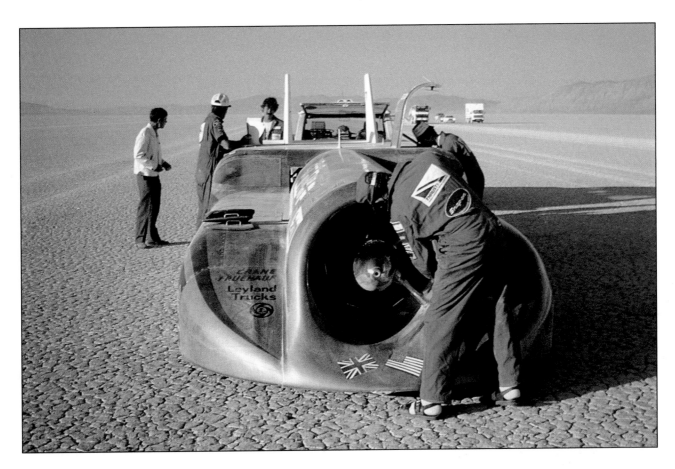

— which occurs in the threshold between subsonic and supersonic — were beginning to make themselves felt.

Up to that point the car had always been run in the early morning, when the air was cold and dense, thus helping the engine produce greater thrust. Now, the team switched to running in the midday heat when the warmer air was less dense and thus created less drag. It was a trade-off of power against drag.

Watched by Gabelich himself, Noble managed 607.903mph (978.115kmh), but his single run seemed to have brought disaster. The Avon engine had overheated badly and severe internal damage was suspected. It was thought that it had been unable to compress all the air it had inhaled and had spewed it back out of its intake instead of the exhaust, in a phenomenon known as 'surging'. If that was the case, getting a spare was virtually impossible. A tense period followed and the entire project hung in the balance until Rolls-Royce sent out its representative, George Webb, from Atlanta. He, to everyone's relief, was able to give the engine a clean bill of health and suggest modifications to the settings to prevent a recurrence of the high temperature problem.

Within days of that alarm Noble managed 622.837mph (1002.144kmh) in one run through the mile as the track dried out following a bout of rain, but a return was prevented when the reheat failed to operate yet again. Thrust 2 was edging up on the record, yet every two steps forward seemed accompanied by one step back.

The reheat problem was finally traced to airlocks in the fuel system created by aeration in the tanks as the car decelerated from a run, and a small timing device was fitted to cure the problem. By 4 October, with the weather at an absolute peak, Noble prepared for another try. His finances were so restricted that seven of his 11 major sponsors had put up enough money for just one more week, and he was already well into that stay of execution.

FINAL RUN

The underside of the car had been polished to a mirror shine to reduce drag, Ackroyd had made small deflectors to mount ahead of the front wheels, to aid streamlining further, and had radically altered the angle of the car to the ground. Normally it ran with its nose down, but this

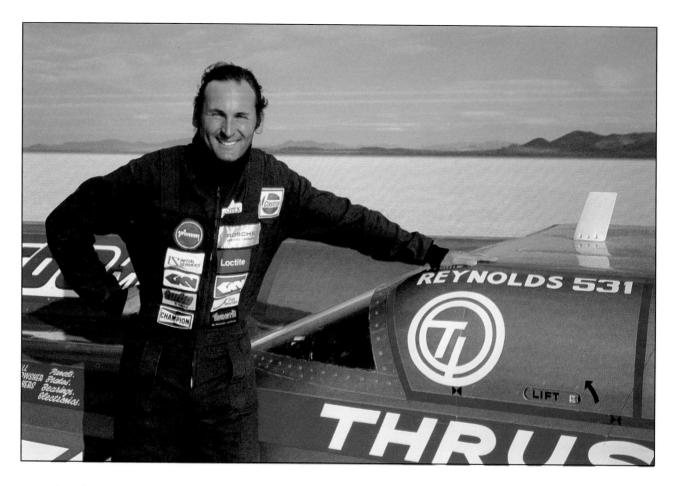

created such enormous suction, or ground effect, that drag was increased. The risk of raising the nose too high was that too much air would get beneath it and might flip the car on to its back over 600 (965), but Ackroyd calculated the parameters and raised the nose a fraction. It was to have a devastating effect.

The tension in the humid air was increased when the Avon refused to fire before the first run. A fuse had blown in the starting system and precious minutes of superb weather were lost as it was hurriedly replaced. Finally, Noble was able to embark on the run he had awaited for nine years.

As soon as Thrust 2 lurched away he engaged the reheat and felt the familiar weaving sensation as the car accelerated at 2G and worked up to the 300mph speeds at which its twin tail fins began to exert their beneficial aerodynamic effect. As Thrust began to run as straight as an arrow, he concentrated solely on keeping it on course, on monitoring his instruments, on extracting the very maximum before deploying his parachutes as gently and accurately as possible and guiding the big, gold stream-

liner to a stop at the southern end of the course, after the most high-pressure minute of his life.

He achieved 624.241mph (1004.403kmh), his fastest speed yet, but it wasn't enough. For his return run, however, he had a longer run-up to the measured distance at the harder end of the track, and the extra momentum as he entered the measured distance would be crucial.

This time his speed was a stunning 642.971mph (1034.540kmh), and the tension was over. The average gave him the new land speed record of 633.468mph (1019.25kmh) and made him the Fastest Man on Earth. It was also an unimpeachable endorsement of John Ackroyd's car, which had been designed to reach 650 (1046). Its official peak during that second run had been 650.88 (1047.26).

After all the years of frustration, scepticism and heartache Project Thrust had finally made it, and its success came not a moment too soon. The following day was hotter still, but the wind was far too high for any runs. And after that the weather was never anywhere near as good again . . .

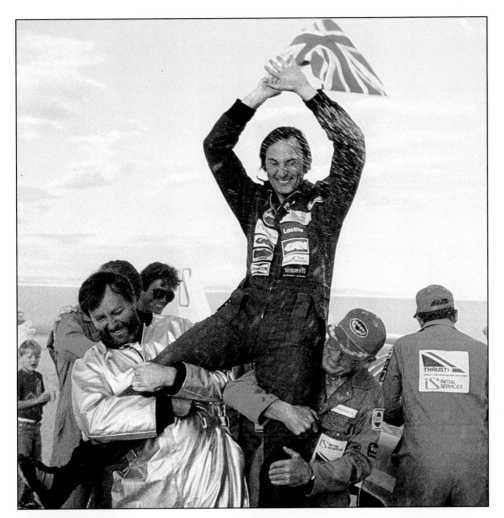

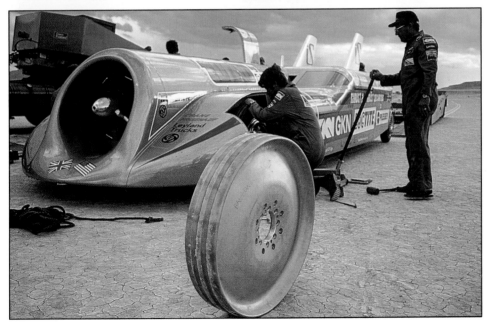

OPPOSITE *Happiness is a Land Speed Record. After nine years Richard Noble achieved his goal, with 633,468mph on October 4 1983. After weeks of awaiting the 'window in the weather', it opened that day. When this photo was taken, the day after, the desert was even hotter and Thrust 2 might thus have gone even faster, except that the wind was high enough to prevent any runs. Fate always did play a big part in Project Thrust . . .*

ABOVE *Immediately after his triumph, Noble is hoisted aloft by his ecstatic crew as he waves the Union Jack. Moments later Ackroyd had the cork popped, and hit Noble squarely in the eye with the first spray of celebratory champagne.*

LEFT *As a tribute to Ackroyd's design genius, precious little of Thrust 2 was ever changed after 1981. The one significant alteration was the move to these six-inch wide front wheels in place of the four-inch versions which proved unstable at Bonneville. He designed Thrust 2 for 650mph, and ultimately it achieved a peak of . . . 650,88.*

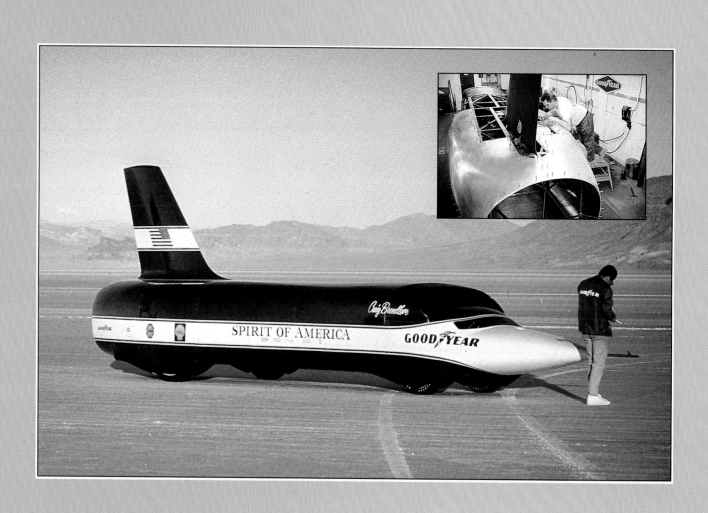

CHAPTER TWO

IN SEARCH OF THE ULTIMATE
— The Land Speed Record

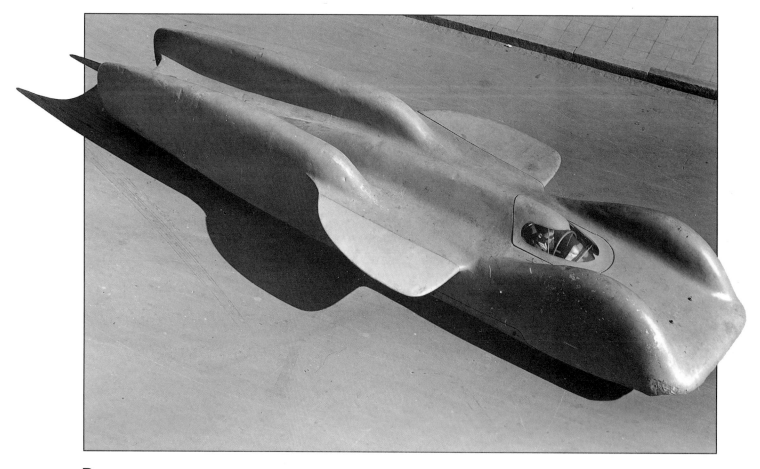

Richard Noble won't be the last man attracted to attempt the Land Speed Record, and he certainly wasn't the first.

When he made his first attempt in 1981, the record's history was a backdrop of triumph and tragedy. 27 men had already succeeded officially in stretching the speed envelope, and had lived to savour the moment. Five hadn't. The quiet Welshman John Godfrey Parry Thomas and Americans Frank Lockhart, Lee Bible, Athol Graham and Glenn Leasher had all pushed too hard and broken through into oblivion.

In the past the danger element had all been part of the thrill. Until the 1920s the record seeker was usually some kind of daredevil to whom the potential rewards were infinitely more attractive than the risk to life and limb was discouraging.

Then came a series of more sober, calculating Englishmen – Henry Segrave, Malcolm Campbell, George Eyston, John Cobb and Donald Campbell. Scientific achievement was everything to them. Attacking the record became not so much a matter of building the most powerful car and then braving it down a beach or across a salt flat, but one of calculating the risks and minimizing them, while accepting them as an integral part of the undertaking. They had no place for death or glory attitudes.

The Land Speed Record has nevertheless always attracted the bold, to whom the challenge of outright speed is much, much more than just a joust of distance against time. Since the invention of the automobile there have always been those willing to push that little bit fur-

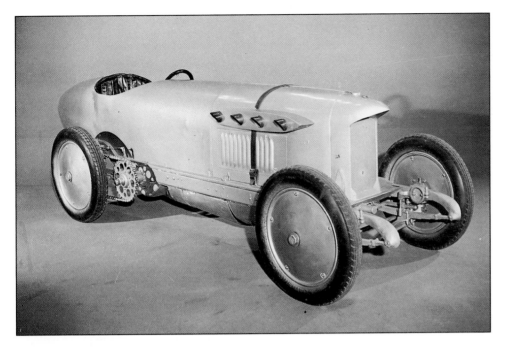

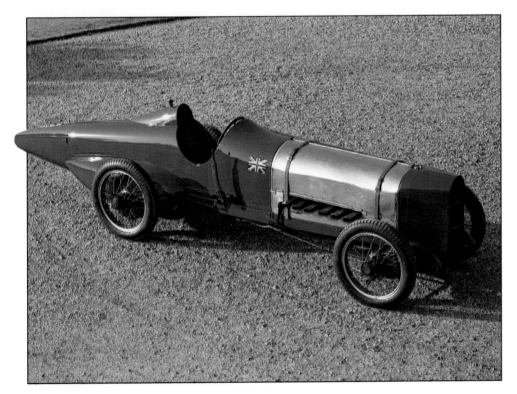

OPPOSITE, ABOVE *Record experts have mixed feelings about the true potential of the Daimler-Benz T80, whose DB603 aero-engine drove all four rear wheels. It was designed by Dr Porsche and Hans Stuck would have driven it, but for Germany's invasion of Poland which started World War Two. Thereafter, the machine never ran.*

ABOVE LEFT *Its predecessor, the 1909 'Blitzen' Benz, proved a highly popular record tool. That year Victor Hemery set a new 125.95mph record with it at Brooklands, before Barney Oldfield achieved 131.27 in it at Daytona four months later. In 1911 Bob Burman achieved 141,37 at Daytona, but like Oldfield, his figure was not recognized in Europe.*

LEFT *Britain bounced back when Kenelm Lee Guinness, heir to the KLG spark plug company, recorded 133.75mph in the 350hp Sunbeam V12 which would later become Malcolm Campbell's first Bluebird record breaker.*

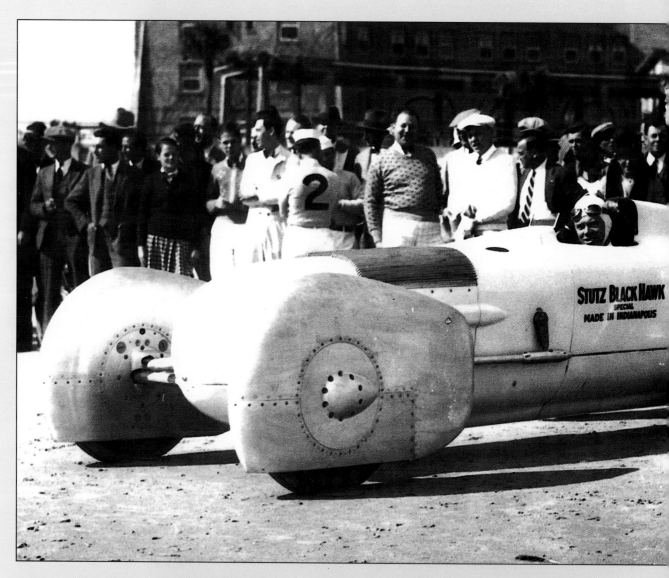

BEAUTY AND THE BEAST

No two contenders better illustrate the disparate approaches to ultimate speed in the twenties than the Black Hawk Stutz and the White Triplex. While one presaged the scientific approach that would become essential in such endeavours, the other was a saurian throwback, an automotive dinosaur. Frank Lockhart could read but barely spell. He was petulant, eschewed small talk and would stop at nothing to bend others to his will. Yet put him in a race car and his touch was brilliantly intuitive. Put him in a workshop and his engineering talents and visions bore the hallmark of genius. Despite his academic shortcomings, he drew streamlined cars while still at school, and further refined the products of the greatest technical brains in American racing.

Those who paid him any attention when he turned up at Indianapolis in 1926 saw him as a brash kid. They thought differently of him when, as a novice, he won the richest race in America. Overnight he became the new hero. For several years he had been winning on the dirt tracks in California, and the Indy win was the icing on the racing cake, but Lockhart wanted something else: the Land Speed Record. The Black Hawk Stutz would swallow all his winnings and more, yet doggedly he persisted. Where typical record cars of the day used giant

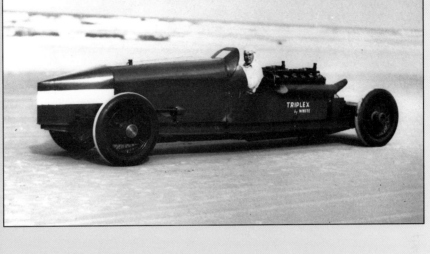

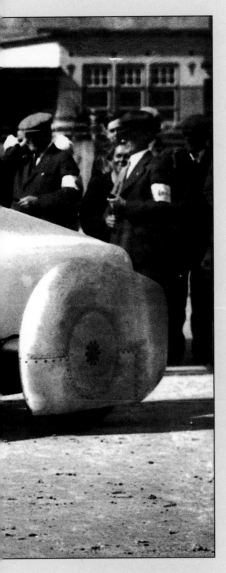

aero-engines in iron girder chassis, Lockhart's theme was lightness and efficiency. Working with the brilliant Weisel brothers, he formulated the Stutz. It was pencil slim, with spats fairing in the wheels, and he pioneered ice cooling instead of using a conventional, drag-inducing water radiator. The 3-litre V16 engine comprised two Miller straight-eights and produced well over 500bhp with super-charging. Two independent assessments gauged its potential well over 280mph (450kmh), at a time when the record had barely scraped past 200 (322).

Against the Stutz as it appeared at Daytona Beach in February 1928 were ranged Malcolm Campbell's Napier-engined Bluebird and Ray Keech's White Triplex. If Bluebird was a lorry in comparison, the Triplex was a locomotive, as crude as the Stutz was beautiful. Crammed into its modified truck chassis were three Liberty V12 aero engines, giving a total of 81 litres and some 1200bhp. One was mounted ahead of the intrepid driver, the remaining two side-by-side behind him. There was no clutch or transmission, the only brakes were on the rear wheels, and sponsor J. M. White of Philadelphia declared streamlining to be bunk. Triplex had a pointed nose and little else. Science met brute force that month, but it was Campbell who snatched the record as the American contenders hit trouble. Running during a squall, in totally unsuitable conditions, Lockhart hit a patch of soft sand and the light Stutz was thrown into the sea. A human chain pulled him to safety, and he vowed to return.

On his run, the abnormally brave Keech was badly scalded when the front engine burst a water hose; there had been no bulkhead to protect him. By late April both contenders had left hospital and were ready to try again. Keech hit 203mph (326kmh), just below Campbell's record, but the timing apparatus failed. Enraged, he then averaged 207.55mph (333.95kmh) to take the record back to America. Lockhart then worked up to the 200mph (322kmh) mark three days later, but the beach was in poor condition. Unable to await improvement, he too reached 203mph (326kmh) and was estimated to be travelling at 225 (362) on his return when a rear tyre burst. The Stutz was thrown down the beach and this time America's non-pareil did not survive. A year later, just after Segrave had smashed the record in the Golden Arrow, Triplex mechanic Lee Bible took over the hot seat to restore American honour. He lifted off too sharply after a fast run and the Triplex hurled itself to destruction as it writhed out of his control. Bible and a photographer perished as the saga of Beauty and the Beast came to its brutal conclusion.

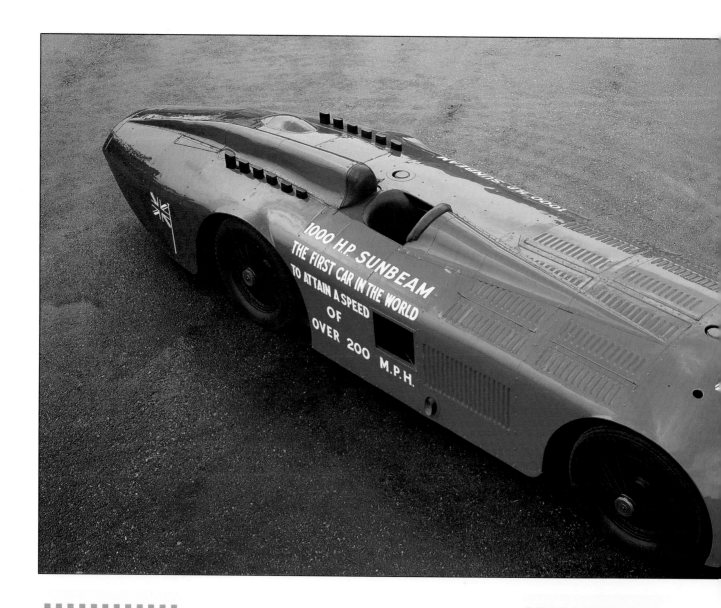

ABOVE *Major Henry Segrave achieved a major milestone in 1927 when in this 1000hp Sunbeam he became the first man ever to travel at 200mph. At Daytona Beach that March, he averaged 203.79mph.*

ther, though the rewards, even for the successful, are few. Pursuit of the record has, at its worst, cost lives, and many other unsuccessful challengers have lost their fortunes and pride. For those who do make it there is little more than a paper certificate and the right to claim that glamorous – and sometimes fleeting – accolade: The Fastest Man on Earth.

That, however, is all part of the spirit of adventure that has driven on the Segraves, Campbells, Eystons, Cobbs, Breedloves, Arfonses, Gabelichs and Nobles in search of the ultimate. It is also what has spurred so many into patriotic action, for national pride has been a cornerstone of most attempts.

Britain's Henry Segrave recaptured the record from

TOP RIGHT *Parry Thomas' engineering genius wrought beneficial changes to Count Zborowsky's Higham Special, which he rechristened Babs. He broke the record twice, but was killed on Pendine Sands in March 1927. Babs was buried there, but exhumed in 1969 by enthusiast Owen Wyn Owen of Capel Curig, who has restored it to full working order.*

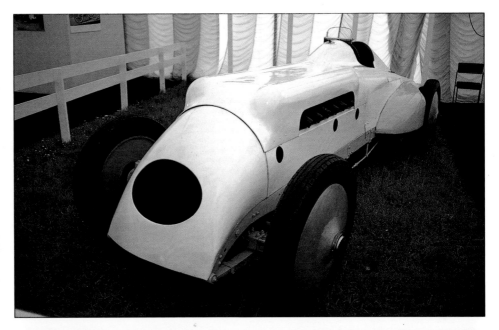

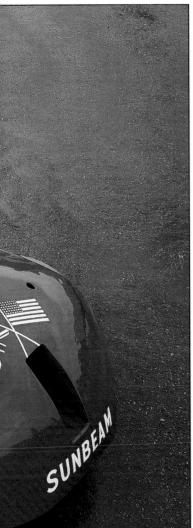

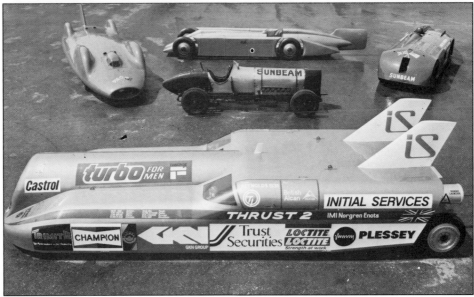

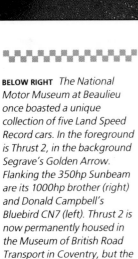

BELOW RIGHT *The National Motor Museum at Beaulieu once boasted a unique collection of five Land Speed Record cars. In the foreground is Thrust 2, in the background Segrave's Golden Arrow. Flanking the 350hp Sunbeam are its 1000hp brother (right) and Donald Campbell's Bluebird CN7 (left). Thrust 2 is now permanently housed in the Museum of British Road Transport in Coventry, but the others continue to reside at Beaulieu.*

American Ray Keech in 1929 – at 231.44mph – in his Golden Arrow, then turned his attention to the water speed record, but was killed shortly after breaking it on Windermere, England, in June 1930. Malcolm Campbell stepped into the limelight the following year with a heavily revised Bluebird. Until 1935, he had doggedly pursued his goal of 300mph (482.7kmh) on land, and finally he succeeded. On the Bonneville Salt Flats, USA in September that year he managed 301.129mph (484.775kmh) and, like his friend and rival Segrave before him, turned to the water.

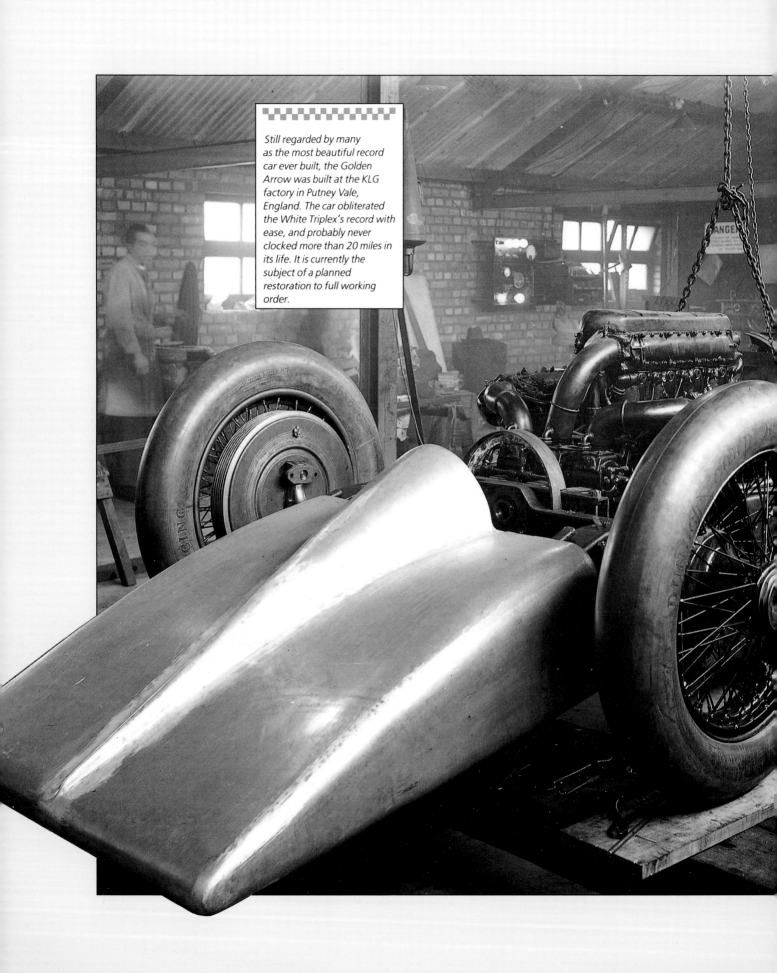

Still regarded by many as the most beautiful record car ever built, the Golden Arrow was built at the KLG factory in Putney Vale, England. The car obliterated the White Triplex's record with ease, and probably never clocked more than 20 miles in its life. It is currently the subject of a planned restoration to full working order.

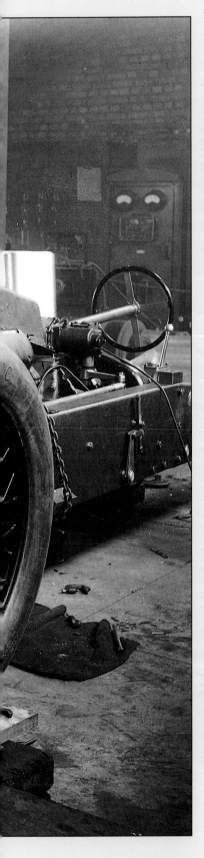

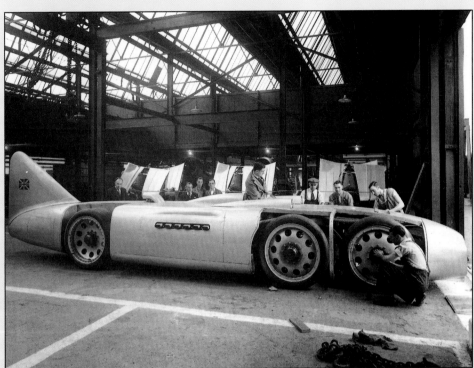

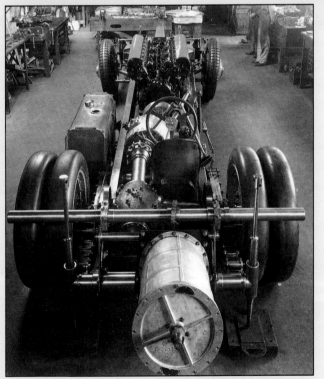

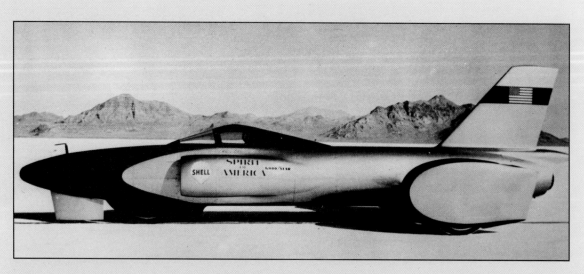

BREEDLOVE'S WILDEST RIDE

Craig Breedlove called his three-wheeled jetcar Spirit of America an automobile, the FIA wasn't sure and ultimately the FIM rated it a motorcycle and sidecar, yet it ended its active life in danger of becoming a speedboat!

In 1963 the Californian had achieved a dream that had already cost him one marriage, when he drove his self-built, jet-propelled tricycle at a speed of 407.45mph (655.58kmh) across the salt flats of Bonneville. His projectile wasn't driven through its wheels and was not therefore an automobile in the eyes of the governing body, yet for the first time a man had driven a two-way average faster than the late John Cobb's 394.20mph (634.26kmh) record which dated back to September 1947. It was the first time any man had pushed past the 400mph (643kmh)

barrier on two runs.

It was the beginning of an explosion of speed that would take the record from 394 (634) to 600mph (965kmh) within two years, after Cobb's mark had stood for 16. Breedlove was content to rest on his laurels for the remainder of 1963, but was stung back into action in October 1964 when Tom Green (413 [664]) then art Arfons (434 [698]) snatched away his title. Arfons had broken his brother's record within three days, yet within a further eight Breedlove had snatched away his honours with 468mph (753kmh). Not satisfied with that, he went out two days later and seared to 526mph (846kmh). As he left the measured mile, however, his braking parachute tore away. Keeping calm he reached for his back-up, but that too failed, leaving him brakeless at 500 (804)! The Spirit blasted down the salt as he burned out

his disc brakes, which were only intended for use below 200 (322). It careered past the end of the course, veered diagonally through a line of telegraph poles, and sheared one as it if were matchwood. Still it didn't slow down, until it ran up and over a bank and vaulted to rest in a brine lake. Breedlove just had time to throw off the cockpit canopy and swim ashore before the racer nosed in, leaving only its tail fin and jetpipe sticking up above the salty surface. Breedlove's crew sped to the accident site, in time to hear him quip hysterically: 'And for my next trick . . . I'll set myself afire!'

At the end of the month Arfons had the last word for the season with 536 (862), but Breedlove was back in 1965 with a new car, the Spirit of America – Sonic 1. And yet again, he survived another high-speed brush with death when the nose lifted over

550mph (885kmh) and he careered, chuteless again, towards the site of his '64 accident. This time he yawed and managed to slow down – and days later he set a new 555mph (893kmh) record.

In their deadly battle, Arfons snapped back with 576 (926), before Breedlove fired the final shot with 600.601mph (966.367kmh). With that, he retired from the game.

ABOVE Breedlove's Spirit of America tricycle was not the first jet car, but it was the first which was successful, taking him to 407, 468 and 526mph between 1963 and 1964.

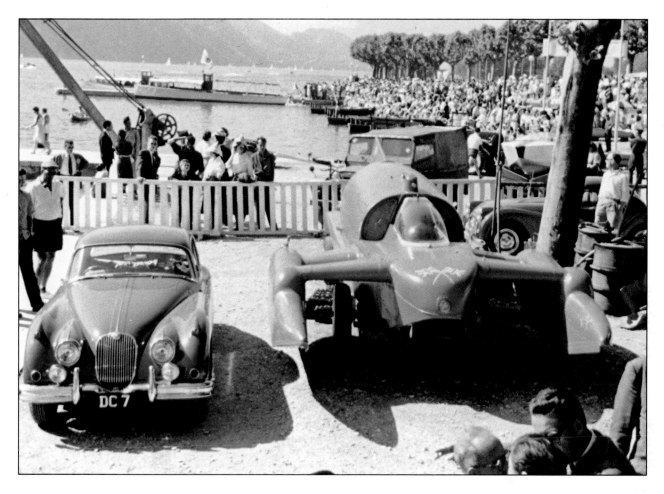

Still the British LSR stranglehold couldn't be broken, as Eyston and Cobb fought their fantastic duel with Thunderbolt and Railton as they headed for 400 (643). Each held the record three times, Eyston at 312 (502), 345 (555) and 357 (574), Cobb at 350 (563), 369 (593) and 394 (633). On his final record he achieved 403mph (648kmh) in one direction, and after that dramatic break-through in 1947 nobody ever went faster until 1960.

By then America had woken up again. When Donald Campbell took his gas turbine-powered Bluebird CN7 to Bonneville in 1960 he faced four American machines. One, the homebuilt City of Salt Lake, killed its over-confident driver Athol Graham. Art Arfons' similar Green Monster, wasn't yet in the top league. With a new car, his time would come.

Mickey Thompson had also built his Challenger in his own backyard, but with its four Pontiac V8s and four-wheel drive it was a cunning device that achieved 406mph (652kmh) in one direction, only to break a drive-shaft on its return.

ABOVE *Donald Campbell was a stickler for detail, and even his roadgoing cars were painted in Bluebird's famous colour. Here in 1959 his Jaguar XK150 sits alongside the K7 hydro-plane in which he was trying to crack 300mph, to arouse interest in a new car to break Craig Breedlove's record, when he died on Coniston Water in January 1967.*

In the Seventies many projects were mooted, but few came to fruition. Typical of the genre was Tony Fox's Proud American, which existed purely in mock-up form. It was displayed at a number of shows and exhibitions and at one time Fox spoke of letting Sammy Miller drive it. The real thing would have been 45 feet long and powered by a hydrogen peroxide rocket giving 35,000 lbs of thrust.

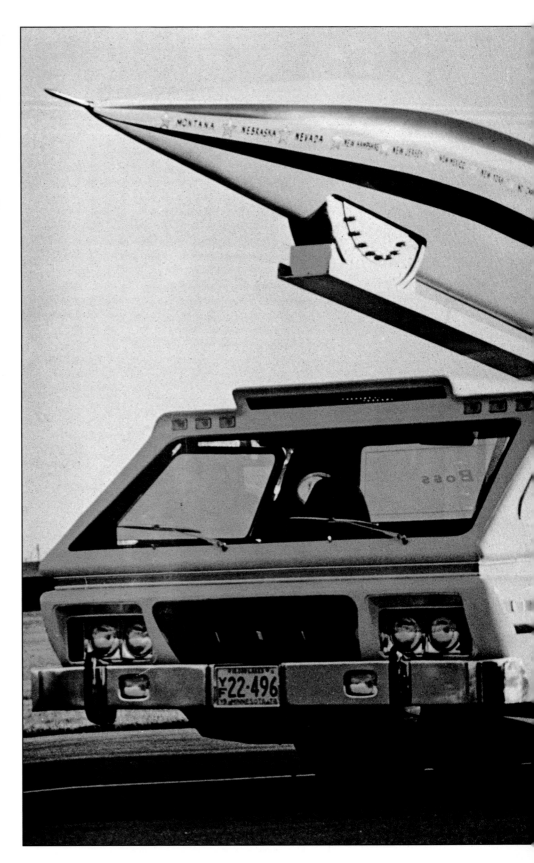

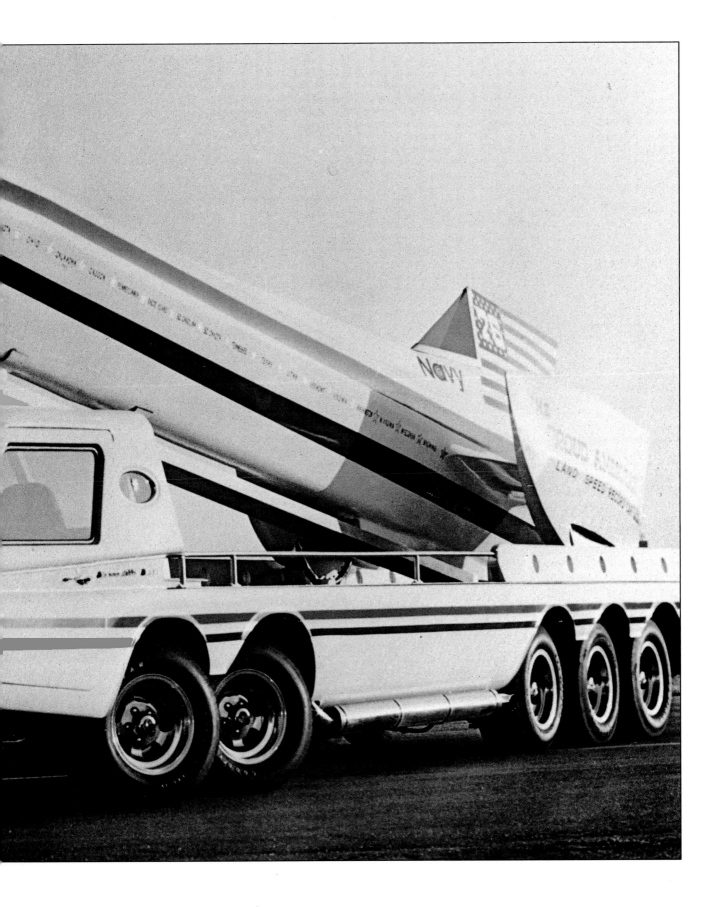

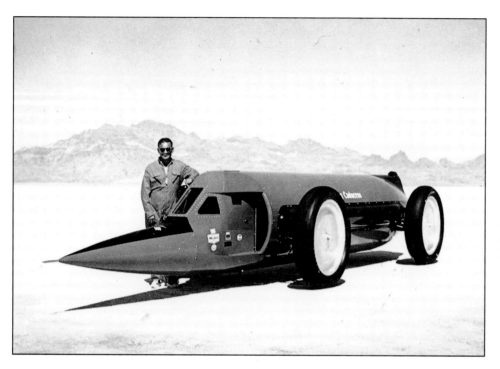

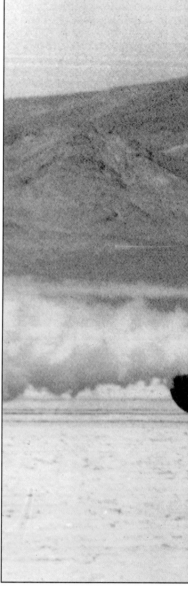

THE JET AGE

It was Nathan Ostich's Flying Caduceus that created the greatest stir, though. The Los Angeles physician had taken a leaf out of the water speed record book by installing a turbojet in a cigar-shaped projectile, and though he was to fail in his efforts, he set a new trend.

Two years later, the impetuous Glenn Leasher went too fast, too soon in his jet-powered Infinity, and was killed as it rolled over at 250mph (402kmh); but the attraction of pure thrust was all too apparent. There was no longer any need for complicated transmissions and

ABOVE *Los Angeles physician Dr Nathan Ostitch was the first to experiment with jet power with his extraordinary Flying Caduceus which ran at Bonneville in 1960. Though he persisted until 1964, he could never coax it above 359mph.*

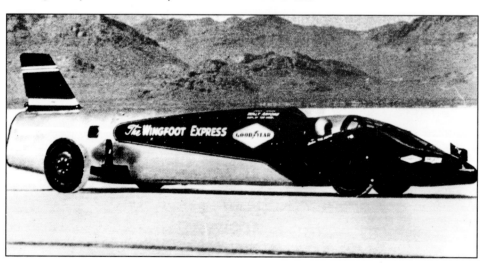

LEFT *Though they were initially dismissed as second raters, Walt Arfons and Tom Green kept on trying and were rewarded with a three-day record of 413.20mph in the Wingfoot Express in 1964.*

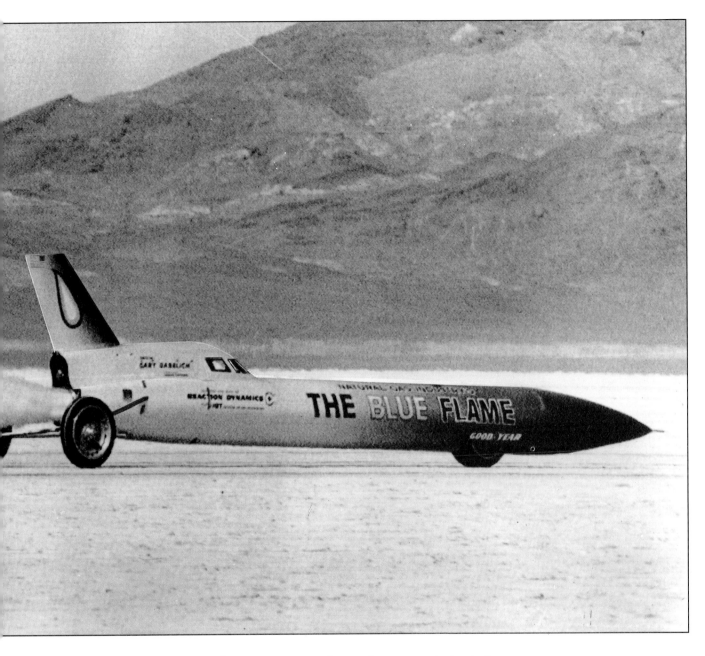

for tyres to transmit massive power. Instead, the new cars were literally blown along by their own exhaust gases.

Those familiar with jet characteristics knew it was only a matter of time, and in August 1963 Craig Breedlove proved them right when he loped to 407.45mph (655.587kmh) in his tricycle Spirit of America. It wasn't an official record since the FIA still required cars to be wheel-driven, but the governing body soon relented to create a new class for thrust vehicles. From Breedlove's historic run onwards, they would be the new outright record setters.

ABOVE *Gary Gabelich's rocket-propelled Blue Flame belches superhot steam as he blasts off on the run that cemented his 622.407mph world record in October 1970. Though it looks like a tricycle, the Flame's two front wheels were mounted very close together.*

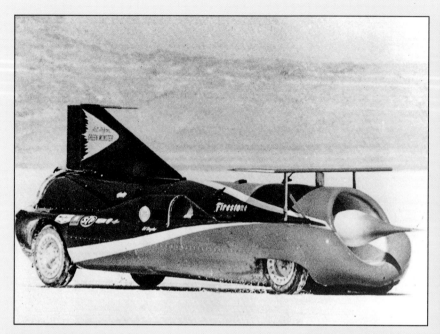

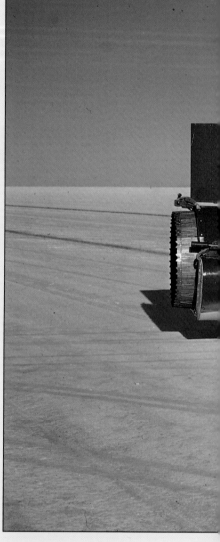

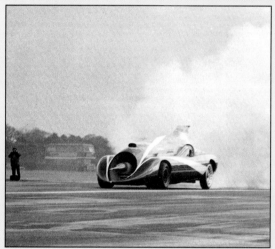

ABOVE *All fins, wings and sonic probes, Art Arfons' Green Monster looked an aerodymamic mess but was one of the cheapest yet effective record cars ever built.*

LEFT *After his 1966 accident, Arfons rebuilt the Monster demonstrated it at Hurn Airport in Bournemouth, England, in 1968.*

ARFONS LOSES HIS BEARINGS

There were a lot of things people couldn't figure out about Art Arfons, 'the junkyard genius of the jet set'. Like Frank Lockhart, he had little formal academic training, yet he was a natural engineer. The giant General Electric conglomerate couldn't work out just how he managed to rebuild one of its J79 turbojet engines which had been run into a steel spike. The company didn't want hot-rodders getting hold of its wares but didn't expect that the damaged surplus unit he obtained would be any use to him, especially as it withheld any workshop manuals.

Arfons calmly stripped it, filed away at the compressor blades and replaced the really damaged ones, and had the engine working well enough to smash the land speed record three times. The experts couldn't comprehend how anything that had cost as little as a reputed $15,000 could be so fast, nor how he had ever persuaded Firestone to invest over $50,000 in building special wheels and tyres for him. Most of all, however, they just couldn't understand how he was still alive on 17 November, 1966 after the 600mph (965kmh)

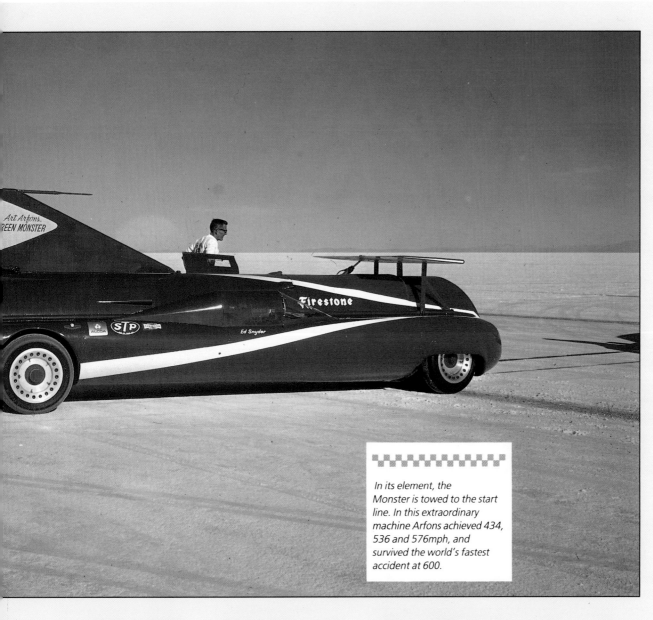

In its element, the Monster is towed to the start line. In this extraordinary machine Arfons achieved 434, 536 and 576mph, and survived the world's fastest accident at 600.

accident that left his Green Monster strewn across 4½ miles (7.2km) of the salt flats at Bonneville. Intent on regaining his record from arch-rival Craig Breedlove, the Akron racer had accelerated to around 610mph (981kmh) when the bearing in the offside front wheel seized and pitched him into a series of end-over-end rolls down the course, scattering bits of the Monster as it went. As his crew rushed screaming to the crash site, Arfons groaned. Incredibly, despite the severity of the accident, which had left the Monster a shattered wreck, Arfons himself was little hurt. 'The worst part was when they started washing the salt out of my eyes,' he recalled. 'That stung like the devil!' Within hours he discharged himself from hospital in Salt Lake City, nursing nothing worse than bruises and facial cuts caused by flying particles of salt, and continued to drive the rebuilt Green Monster in demonstration runs. Incredibly, in 1989 this sprightly and devil-may-care grandfather was building a new, superlight contender, with the intention once again of becoming the Fastest Man on Earth.

Tom Green became the first man officially to break the record with a jet when he took the Wingfoot Express to 413mph (664kmh) in October 1964, but his glory lasted only three days before Art Arfons, brother of the Wingfoot's builder Walt, initiated an orgy of speed that made Campbell's 403mph (648kmh) in Bluebird that July actually look paltry.

As Breedlove and Art Arfons indulged in their dangerous game of Russian roulette throughout 1965, the record nudged over 600 with Breedlove's final 600.601mph (966.367kmh), and that set the scene for one of the most remarkable and scientific projects of them all, the Blue Flame.

Unlike the majority of contenders over the past 50 years, the pencil-slim Flame was built entirely for the record, right down to its innovative hydrogen peroxide and liquified natural gas-fuelled rocket engine. In a quite remarkable display, given the newness of its technology (and the fact that pilot Gary Gabelich had to quell a minor mutiny at one stage as Bonneville ennui began to affect his crew), the Reaction Dynamics team spent a month on the salt from mid-September 1970 and came away on 23 October with a brand new record at 622.407mph (1001.452kmh), even though the Flame never ran with more than 16,000 (7264) of its 22,000lbs (9988kg) of thrust.

In subsequent years the challengers came to Bonneville, but left empty-handed. Slick Gardner broke new ground by trying solid aluminium wheels on Art Arfons' rebuilt Green Monster, but gave up when the handling gave him the chills, while Kitty O'Neill and Hal Needham both went fast in Bill Fredrick's rocket-powered SMI Motivator, although scepticism still exists over their claimed 638mph (1026kmh) performances, and neither was official. That project would lead to the most controversial of all, the Budweiser Rocket, which is said to have achieved the Sound Barrier but was never timed by anything approaching FISA-approved equipment (see page 62 for details of speed claimed).

THE FUTURE

The days when the Land Speed Record had any relevance to everyday motoring had by then long gone. Now, challenging it has become a corporate budget project that demands a great deal of financial and physical support allied to highly sophisticated technical equipment and back-up. Now that man has reached deep into space

ACCELERATION UNLIMITED

If his own Land Speed Record aspirations look weaker each year, Sammy Miller nonetheless is the fastest accelerating man in the world.

Using a series of Funny Car dragsters powered by hydrogen peroxide rocket motors, and all named Vanishing Point, the New Jerseyman has performed some incredible feats. How about 0 to 60mph in 0.28 seconds, or 0 to 100 in 0.36? Or the standing eighth mile in 1.606 at a terminal speed of 319mph and the quarter mile in 3.58 at 386?

In the tight confines of a drag strip, that is real speed, and he has given similar performances in his open-wheeled rocket car Oxygen. As if that isn't enough, in February 1981 he achieved 247mph (397kmh) in 1.6 seconds on Lake George in New York State – running the second Vanishing Point on skis across the frozen surface!

Piston-engined, wheel-driven machinery can't compete with such velocities, but are still incredibly fast. In 1975 legendary drag racer Don Garlits broke through the 250mph (402kmh) speed barrier for the quarter mile. Joe Amato took that to 260 (402) nine years later, and then Garlits replied with 270mph

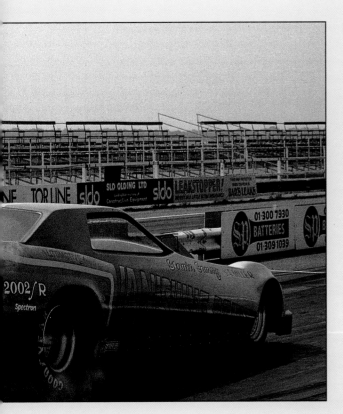

chasing the Sound Barrier on land has lost its impact for some. But space is an intangible, its successful conquests remote. The record remains touchable.

It still throws out a challenge, and remains a story of human endeavour and courage. The Machine costs Money, and only that will ever place it on the salt or desert. But only the Man within it can guide it to success or failure. And therein lies the real charm of the Land Speed Record, one of the most prestigious, dangerous and costly challenges left to man.

Will anyone challenge Noble's 633.468mph (1019.25kmh) figure?

Upon his return to Britain in October 1983, he was already making contingency plans for Thrust 3, a car to spear beyond the Sound Barrier. 'All we need is the challenge, someone to beat our record, and then we can come back and have another go!' he enthused.

But though several respected names have publicized plans for attempts, nobody has gone back to the Black Rock Desert or Bonneville in the intervening years.

Land Speed Record attempts require vast sums of money, and while many hungry challengers have the capability and courage to light the rocket or slam the jet engine into afterburner, that is a part of the equation that only becomes relevant once the pilot has found the backing to build his car. Without the finance to proceed – and the amount of money involved increases year by year – none is ever likely to do more than dream of seeing the earth's curvature from inside of a projectile.

In 1983 veteran speedking Craig Breedlove built a full-scale mock-up of his proposed Spirit of America – Sonic 2, with which he would erase Noble's record, but went no further.

Rocket-powered drag racer Sammy Miller remains confident he can blast to a new mark, but has been without visible sign of progress since 1982. In Colorado, Bill Gaynor continues to build his ungainly City of Sterling in the hope of fulfilling his ambition.

In Australia, Rosco McGlashan works to find the finance for his Aussie Invader. Of them all, he has been talking for the shortest time and therefore probably stands the best chance of reaching the salt.

As Noble said when he started Project Thrust, 'Record attempts require Dedication, Determination and Money, in that order'. At present nobody in the world seems genuinely close to combining all three requirements in any one project. But one day somebody, somewhere, will.

(434kmh) in 1986. However, Darrell Gwynne deprived him of his glory later that year with an elapsed time of 5.26 seconds for the standing start quarter, at a speed of 278mph (447.3kmh). That heralded an explosion of speed in the NHRA series, as first Amato and then Eddie Hill took the act over 280mph (450kmh). The record is based on elapsed time, and Hill set a new mark of 4.973 seconds (287mph [462kmh]) at Houston in October 1988. At the same meeting he had achieved an unofficial 4.93 seconds (288mph [463kmh]); at the same venue earlier in the year he set an unofficial speed record of 291.72mph [493.37kmh]. The fastest electrically-powered car is Roger Hedlund's Battery Box, which achieved an average of 175.061mph (281.67kmh) for two flying start runs across Bonneville in 1974.

FATHER AND SON – THE CAMPBELLS

There has never been a record-breaking family quite like the Campbells, Malcolm and son Donald. Malcolm, who began his record-breaking career as Captain Campbell and was knighted for his 1931 success, was a hard-nosed diamond merchant and insurance expert of awesome courage and determination. Nothing, but nothing, ever stood between him and his goals for long.

In his early exploits with the ex-Lee Guinness 350bhp Sunbeam he exceeded the official record more than once, only to be denied it on technicalities. The disappointments simply fanned his fire and finally he succeeded for the first time in 1924, with 146mph (234kmh). Eleven years later he had set his ninth land speed record – nearly double anyone else's tally – and was the Fastest Man on Earth at 301mph (484kmh). Even when he had run out of challengers to beat, he kept chipping away until he achieved that final goal; and then immediately looked elsewhere to win four records on water.

While Sir Malcolm was tough, overbearing and sometimes even cruel, son Donald was totally different. Forever in his father's shadow, he took up his mantle only when

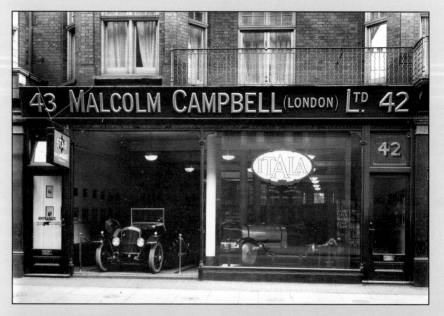

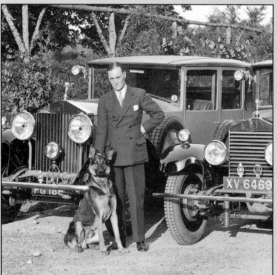

ABOVE *Malcolm Campbell was a successful businessman as well as record breaker, running his own car sales company.*

LEFT *Success as a diamond merchant and insurance underwriter brought further trappings of wealth, a luxurious home and a brace of Rolls-Royces.*

the Old Man died in December 1948. Donald concentrated at first on the prewar Bluebird hydroplane. After countless disappointments he lost his fight to stop the Americans taking his father's last speedboat record, and then lost the

boat itself; but between 1955 and 1959 he went on to set six water speed records in a new jet-powered Bluebird. And then came the Bluebird car. If Donald was a gentler man than his father, he possessed the same sense of grandeur.

Bluebird had to be the biggest and the best. He took it to Bonneville in 1960, and promptly crashed it by trying to go too fast for his own experience. He was lucky to survive the 360mph (579kmh) flip: but he also had his father's courage,

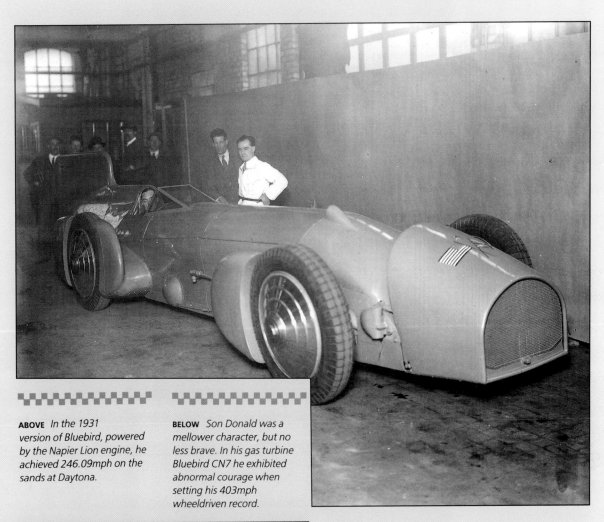

▬▬▬▬▬▬▬▬▬▬▬   ▬▬▬▬▬▬▬▬▬▬▬

ABOVE *In the 1931 version of Bluebird, powered by the Napier Lion engine, he achieved 246.09mph on the sands at Daytona.*

BELOW *Son Donald was a mellower character, but no less brave. In his gas turbine Bluebird CN7 he exhibited abnormal courage when setting his 403mph wheeldriven record.*

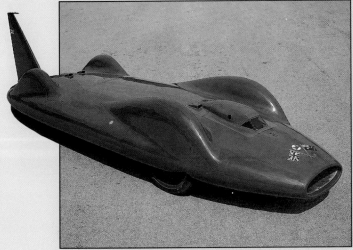

and came back with a new version.

From 1962 to July 1964 he was dogged by awful weather on Australia's Lake Eyre, but finally wrestled the CN7 to 403mph (648kmh) on a track through which the giant car punched massive ruts. For all his bravery, it was a hollow victory. Breedlove had gone faster the previous year and nobody cared whether his car played by the rules or not. Bluebird was a White Elephant.

As if to prove a point, Campbell set his seventh water record on the last day of 1964 and began planning a new rocket car to break the Sound Barrier. He was trying for his eighth boat record on Coniston Water, England on 4 January, 1967, to raise finance for the project, when Bluebird took off at more than 300mph (482kmh) and somersaulted to destruction. His body was never found.

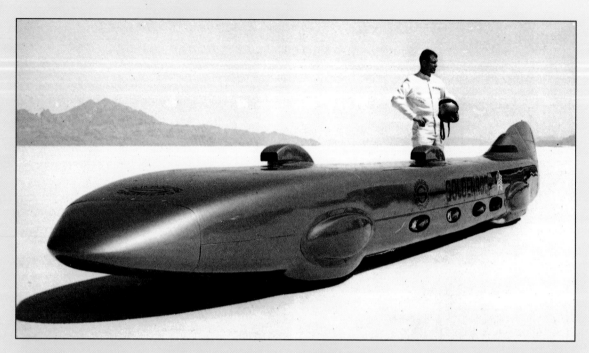

THE RULES

On paper, attempting the Land Speed Record looks straightforward, even easy. You build the most powerful car you can, take it somewhere flat, and keep the throttle to the floor over a measured distance. Then you turn round and do it again and the average gives you a new record.

There are very few limitations on design, and the rules are straight-forward, but that hasn't stopped several contenders bypassing them when it has suited them. However, for records to receive official ratification from the sport's governing body the FISA (the sporting arm of the FIA *Fédération Internationale de l'Automobile*), they must comply fully with what regulations it does lay down.

Attempts must take place on level courses that have been surveyed by recognized bodies. The equipment used to time the runs must be of acceptable standard and quality, and must be used by independent timekeepers from a national club affiliated to the FISA. As the majority of runs are made on American soil, this usually means USAC (United States Auto Club).

The actual Land Speed Record is the official average of the *times* of two consecutive runs, one in each direction, through a measured mile or kilometre, the mile being the most widely recognized distance. The runs must be completed

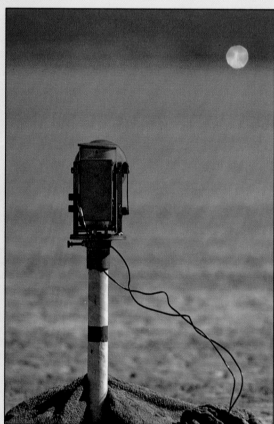

within one hour, and the overall speed is then computed from the average elapsed time, not the average speeds.

As speeds have pushed to 600mph (965kmh) and beyond, a minimum course length is around 13 miles (20.9km), which naturally limits the choice of venues. The measured mile is sited in the middle, to give the driver an equal distance at either end of the course in which to accelerate and decelerate on each run.

Land Speed Record contenders must have at least four wheels and at least two of them must be steered. The cars may be driven by pure-thrust jet or rocket power, must remain in contact with the ground to all intents and purposes, and are not allowed to use aerodynamic devices which the driver can move when he is sitting in the cockpit. All aerodynamic adjustments must be made before a run.

The most celebrated case of rule bypassing was the Budweiser Rocket, which was timed at an alleged 739.666mph (1190.122mkh) in December 1979. Its speed, which it was said broke the Sound Barrier, was measured by non-sanctioned radar, over a one-way distance of only 52.8ft, and was thus not recognized as any kind of official mark by FISA even though those involved claimed it as a new record.

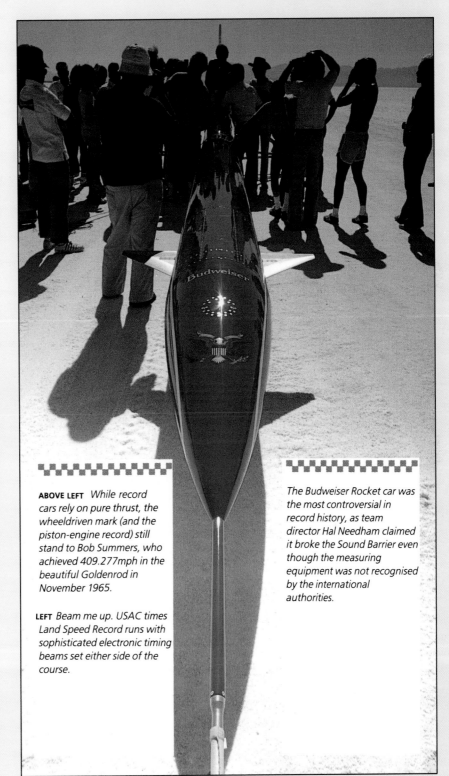

ABOVE LEFT *While record cars rely on pure thrust, the wheeldriven mark (and the piston-engine record) still stand to Bob Summers, who achieved 409.277mph in the beautiful Goldenrod in November 1965.*

LEFT *Beam me up. USAC times Land Speed Record runs with sophisticated electronic timing beams set either side of the course.*

The Budweiser Rocket car was the most controversial in record history, as team director Hal Needham claimed it broke the Sound Barrier even though the measuring equipment was not recognised by the international authorities.

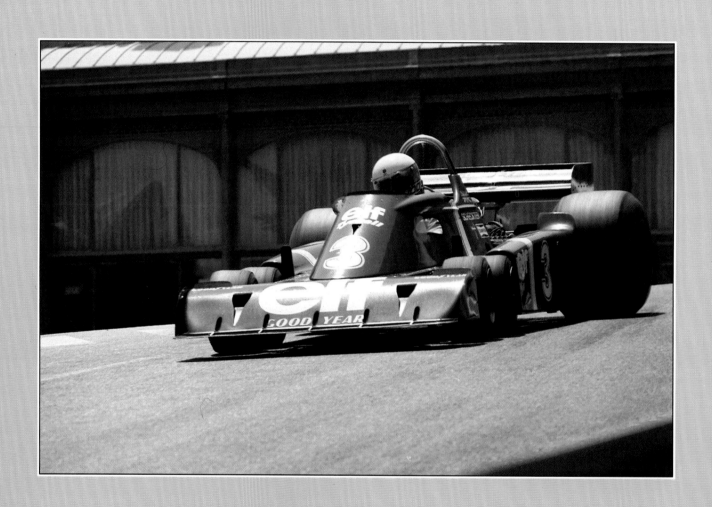

CHAPTER THREE

FURTHER, FASTER, LONGER

– Developments in Motor Sport

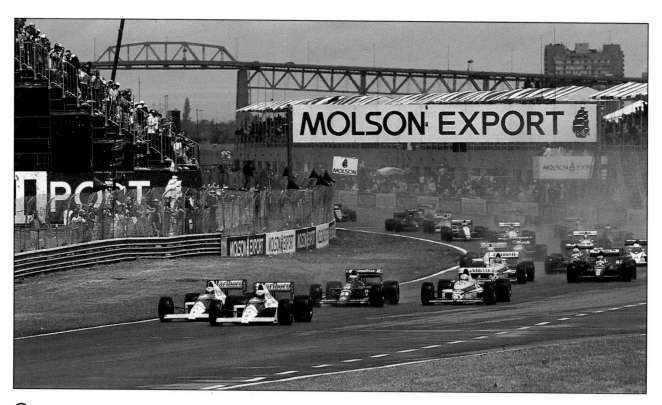

Once, motor racing was purely a sport, conducted by gentlemen wealthy enough to indulge themselves. When advertising in motorsport was permitted in Europe from 1968, purists threw up their hands in horror and bemoaned the arrival of the commercial age.

Now, motorsport is a highly visual marketing medium, but the idea of exploiting that for gain is nothing new. After all, the Nazi government did just that in the 1930s when it used the sledgehammer successes of Mercedes-Benz and Auto Union to extol its own political strength and technical superiority.

The immediate postwar years gave sporting instincts another chance, but while some hail the 1950s as the good old days, the truth is that the depth of competition was nothing like as strong as it is today in the Grand Prix arena, and that decade's one real legacy to development was the advance of the rear-engined racer. John Cooper's early British cars had been laughed at initially, but by the end of the 1950s they were the championship winners, and took Jack Brabham comfortably into the 1960s as well.

What the rear-engined cars brought was superior handling balance, and before long the new 1.5-litre F1 cars were lapping faster than their old 2.5-litre counterparts had. When the 3-litre formula came in for 1966,

the monocoque chassis was the major development, courtesy of the brilliance of Colin Chapman of Lotus, but the cars were essentially larger-engined versions of earlier designs. However, by the time the formula was amended in late 1986 to increase the capacity of normally aspirated cars to 3.5-litres, the face of the racing car had changed beyond recognition. Undoubtedly, the 3-litre formula bequeathed the greatest number of significant technological experiments and advances of any formula category.

TURBINE POWER

The arrival of the 3-litre F1 coincided with an exciting challenge to the supremacy of the piston engine, in the form of the gas turbine. It had been around for some years, and the first racing car to be powered by one was the Grancor Special built by Kurtis Kraft in 1950 for the Granatelli Corporation. It raced initially with piston engines — and actually finished second in the Indianapolis 500 in 1952 — but when a Boeing 502 turbine was installed the following year it wasn't fast enough.

Eight years later sportsman and racing car builder John Zink installed another Boeing turbine in the rear of his spaceframe chassis, but it proved difficult to sort out and the car failed to qualify for the 1962 500 despite the

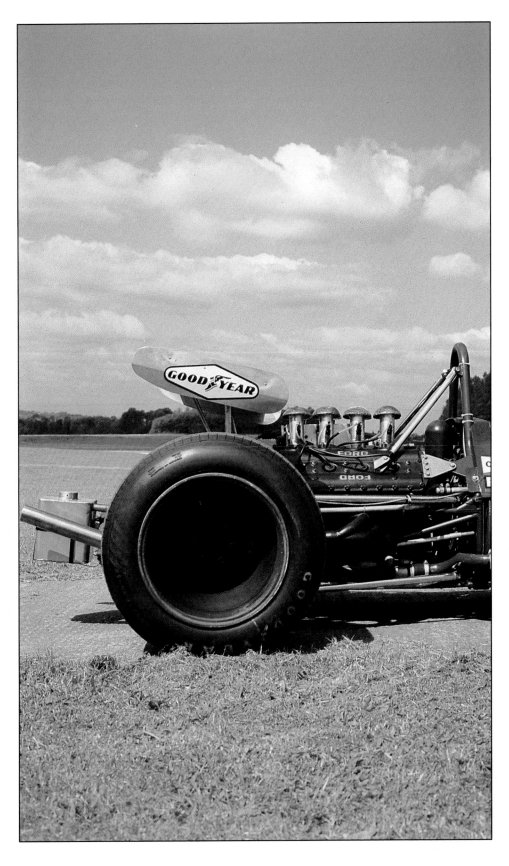

OPPOSITE *Motor racing in the late Eighties had developed into a hi-tech sport almost totally dependent for its prosperity on vast injections of sponsorship. That requirement is reflected by the billboard appearance of this F1 field, on which even the poorest team's cars boast some commercial allegiance. Here Prost leads Senna in the 1989 Canadian GP.*

LEFT *The Sixties changed the face of Grand Prix racing for ever, when Ferrari and Brabham (whose BT26 is illustrated here) introduced aerofoil wings to generate downforce at the 1968 Belgian GP.*

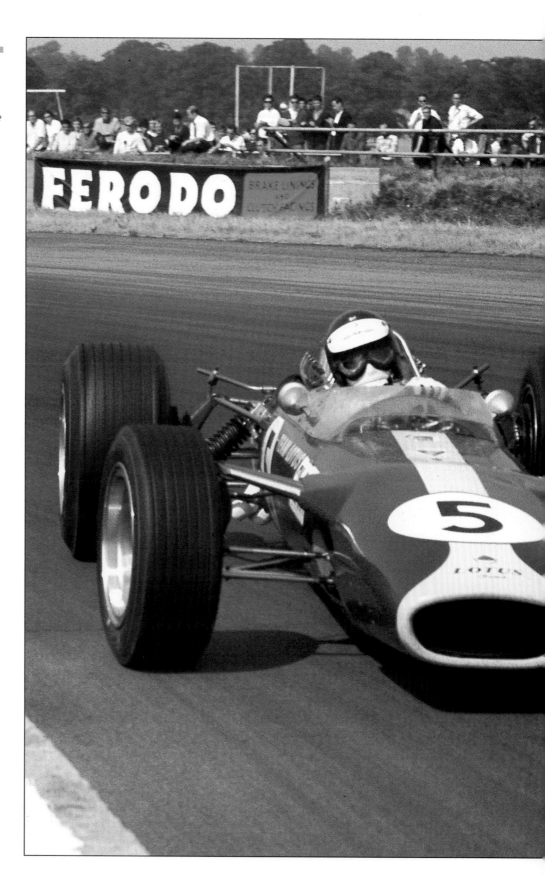

Before wings and slick tyres glued them to the road and dramatically reduced braking distances, racing cars could be cornered extravagantly without serious penalty. Here Jim Clark thrills spectators at Silverstone in 1967, the year before the aerodynamic revolution took over.

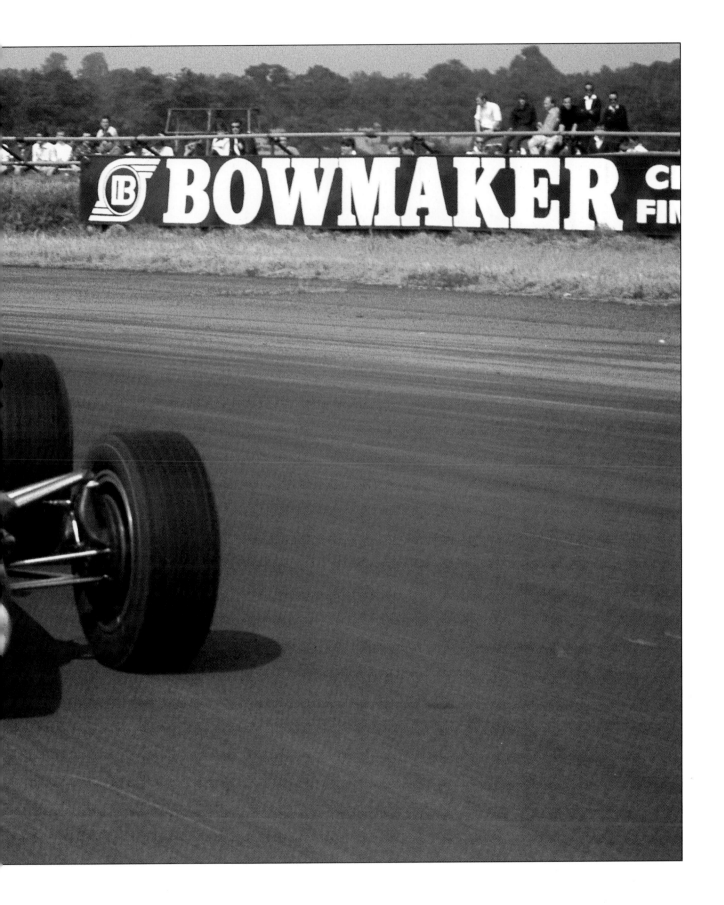

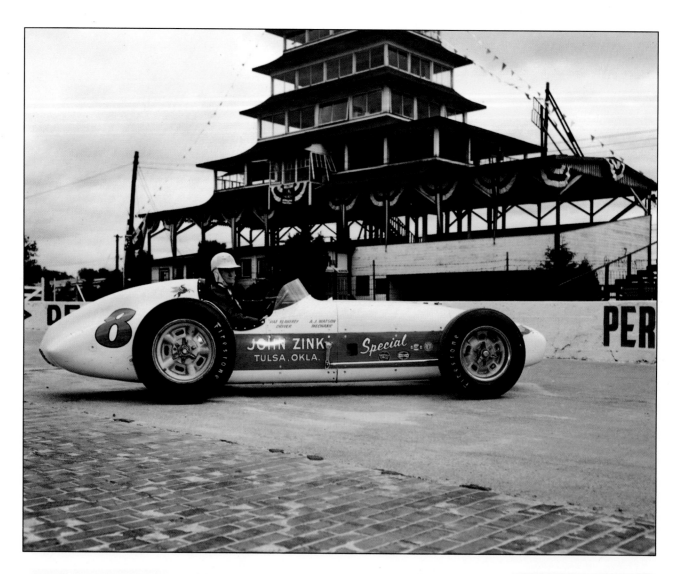

ABOVE John Zink achieved a double ambition when Pat Flaherty drove this John Zink Special to victory at 128.490mph in the 1956 Indianapolis 500 classic, to duplicate Bob Sweikert's similar success the previous year. Before long, Zink would begin eyeing a new source of power with which he hoped to supplant his roadster's Offenhauser piston engine.

talent of Dan Gurney at the wheel. As far as the sporting world was concerned, turbine cars weren't really taken seriously.

In Britain, Rover had experimented successfully with one of its own turbines installed in a two-seater sports car chassis designed by BRM, and had covered sufficient distance to finish seventh and 10th at Le Mans in 1963 and 1965. Nevertheless, the car wasn't really competitive, though it was at least reliable.

Attitudes to turbines changed abruptly in 1967, when Parnelli Jones came within three laps of winning the Indy 500 before a $5 bearing failed. He had a lap lead on A. J. Foyt, who went on to win.

Jones' car was the STP Paxton turbocar, which created a sensation in the conservative world of United States Auto Club racing. It used an X-shaped aluminium back-

RIGHT In 1962, the Tulsa businessman sponsored the construction of the Boeing turbine-engined Zink Trackburner Special. It was to have been driven by Dan Gurney, Duane Carter and Bill Cheesbourg; though it failed to find the speed necessary to qualify for the 500, it started a new trend.

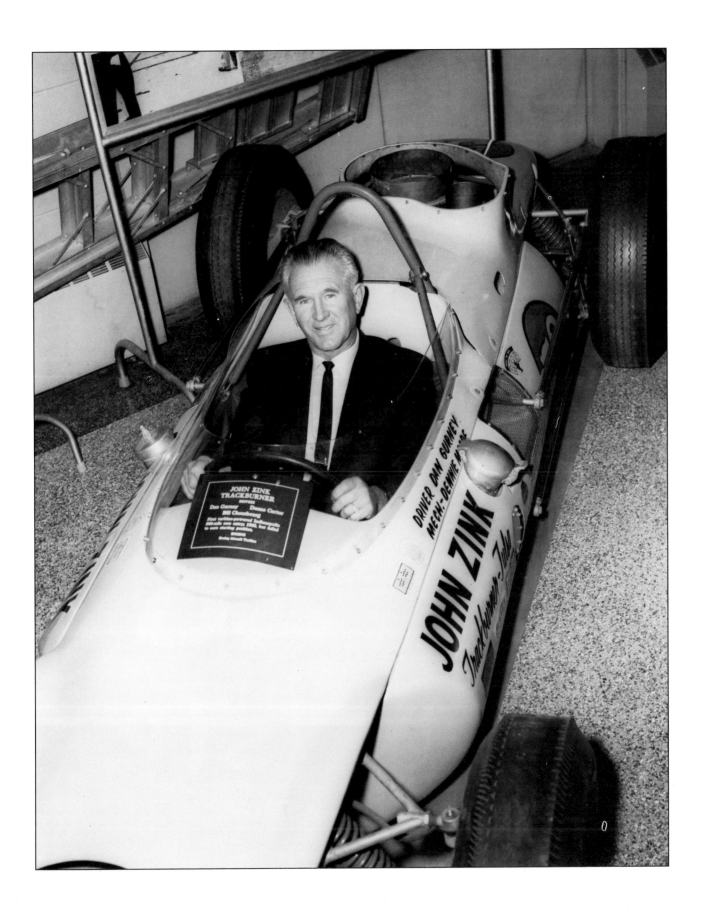

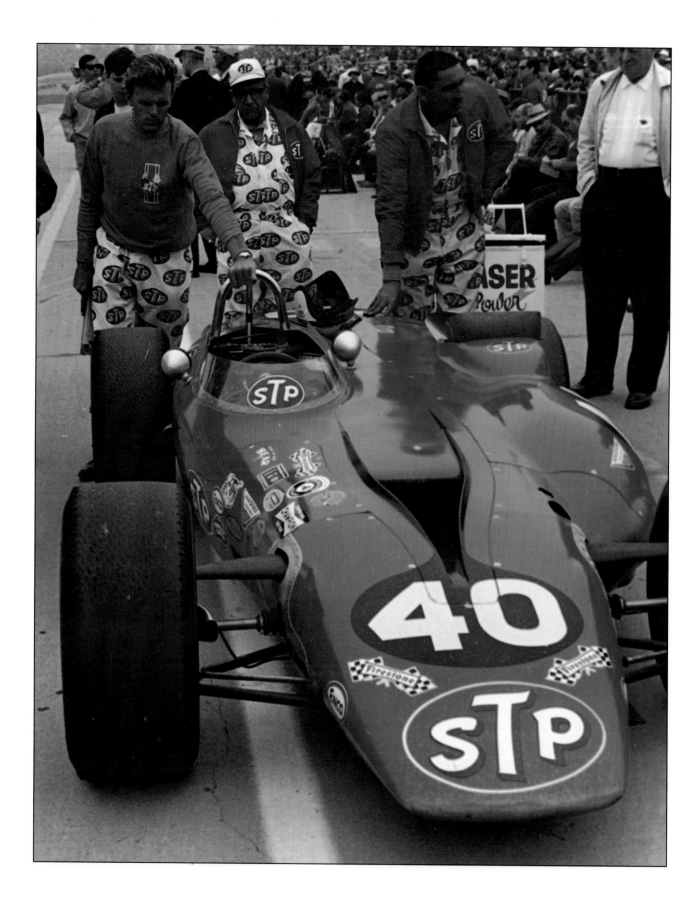

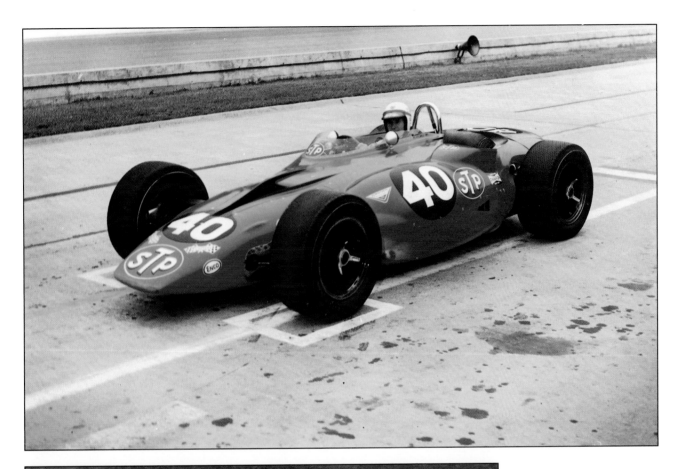

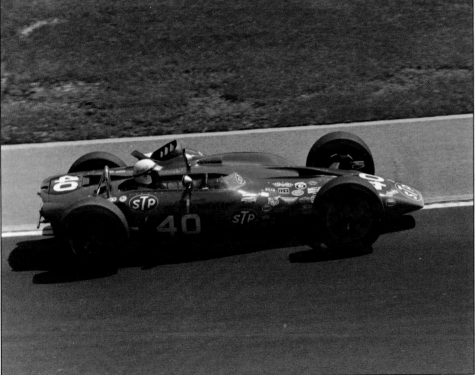

OPPOSITE *STP boss Andy Granatelli was always a colourful thinker. He was also the first man successfully to employ the gas turbine engine at Indianapolis with this 1967 contender.*

ABOVE *Rufus Parnelli Jones, rated by knowledgeable insiders as the best Champcar driver of all time, was selected as the driver of the STP Paxton turbine, which used a modified Pratt & Whitney engine mounted to his left.*

LEFT *Jones' speed on raceday stunned observers and terrified the establishment, but many overlooked the advantage conferred by his car's four-wheel drive. He led until three laps from the finish, when a $5 bearing failed.*

RIGHT *Officialdom was always intrigued by the STP Paxton turbocar. After Jones' sensational performance it was even more interested, and lost no time in reducing the permissible turbine intake area, fearing the piston engine would be outdated overnight. Granatelli, here demonstrating the air brake, eventually took legal action.*

OPPOSITE *The Howmet Corporation ran this prototype turbine sports car in the 1968 Championship, including the Le Mans race at which it is pictured. It met with little success.*

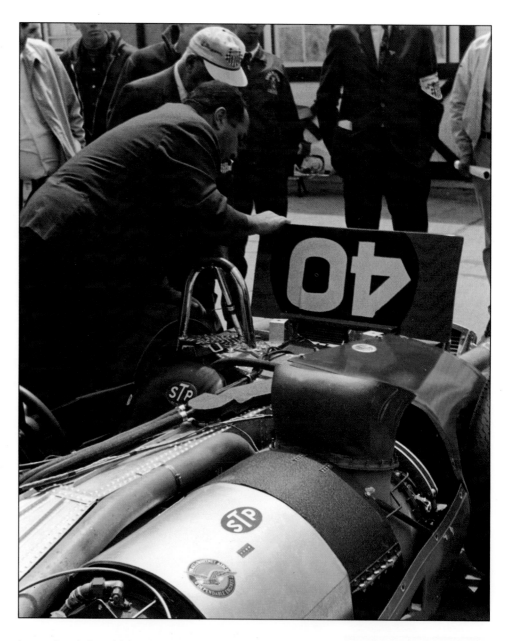

bone chassis in which Jones sat on the right, alongside a 550bhp Pratt and Whitney ST-6 turbine, taken from a snowplough. It used a constant-mesh gearbox and four-wheel drive, and even though the engine wasn't even tuned, had no trouble qualifying sixth fastest at 166.075mph (267.714kmh), only 3mph (4.8kmh) slower than the polewinner.

From the first lap of the 200-lap event, Jones was leading and was seven seconds ahead when the race was stopped by rain. When it was restarted the following day the 'whooshmobile' swept straight back into the lead until that critical moment when a bearing in the gearcase

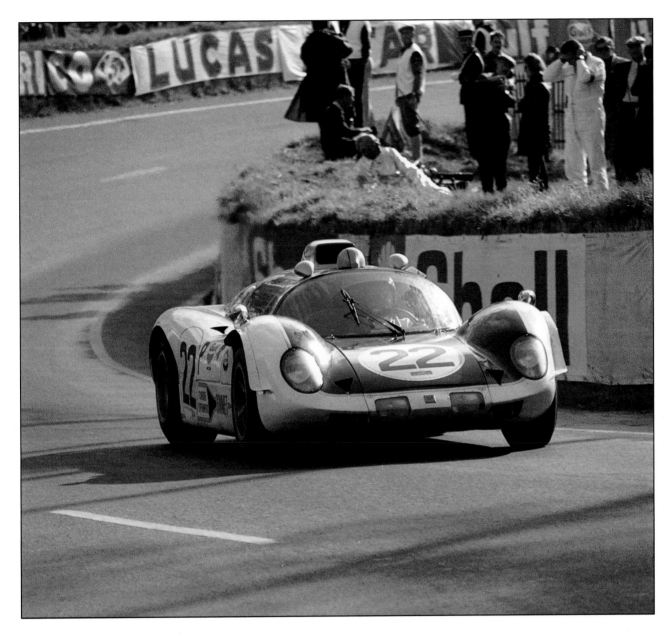

broke up. 'I still get sick just to think about it,' grimaced Jones 21 years later.

The speed of the turbine shocked everyone, not least the Granatelli Corporation's rivals and the USAC board. Instantly the latter slapped a limit on the intake size of the engines, fearing that, just as the rear-engined racers had rendered the old front-engined roadsters obsolete overnight, so the turbines would kill the piston engines.

USAC's overreaction overlooked the advantage of the turbocar's four-wheel drive system, and its cunning weight distribution; as far as it was concerned its speed was purely down to the turbine. It introduced a new intake limit of 23.9 sq in (60.7 sq cm), but then slashed that to 15.999 (40.637) when it learned that the turbine had run happily at 21.9 sq in (55.6 sq cm) in the race.

While Andy Granatelli took USAC to court over its new rulings – and lost – he was also working with Colin Chapman and Lotus to build an all-new turbine for the 1968 race. When the Lotus 56 appeared it caused another sensation with its wedge shape, and while it used a Pratt and Whitney 70 series engine mounted behind the driver, it was also much lighter than the STP Paxton car.

British driver Mike Spence was killed testing a 56 at Indianapolis in May, exactly a month after Jim Clark had

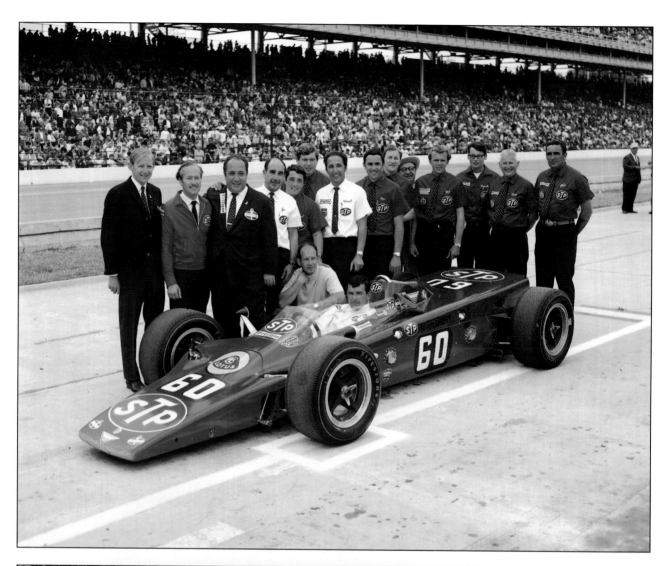

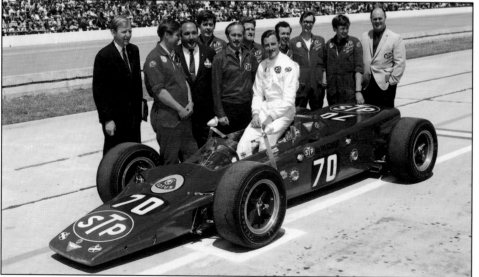

ABOVE *Red Wedge: After the STP Paxton turbocar, Colin Chapman's Lotus 56 became Granatelli's riposte. He and Chapman are second and third from left, while Joe Leonard poses for the traditional pole-winner's picture. The retired Parnelli Jones kneels by the cockpit.*

LEFT *Britain's Graham Hill, winner of the controversial 1966 Indy 500, poses with Chapman in the car he placed in the middle of the front row for the 1968 race.*

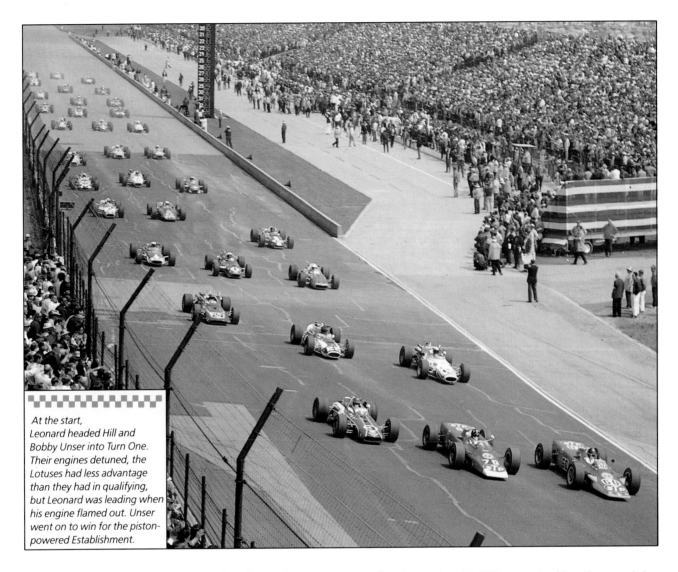

At the start, Leonard headed Hill and Bobby Unser into Turn One. Their engines detuned, the Lotuses had less advantage than they had in qualifying, but Leonard was leading when his engine flamed out. Unser went on to win for the piston-powered Establishment.

been killed, and that left Graham Hill and Americans Joe Leonard and Art Pollard to fly the STP Lotus flag in the race. Leonard had savaged the piston cars in qualifying with a four-lap pole-winning average of 171.953mph (276.672kmh), a new record. Hill sat alongside him, with 171.208 (275.473). With special tuning the cars had around 500bhp to play with, compared to the turbo-charged piston-engined cars' 650–750bhp, but their handling and downforce proved so advantageous they were able to parlay it into superior lap speeds.

Just as Jones had the previous year, so Leonard swept into the lead on race day, but this time the high ambient temperature handicapped the turbines in their 480bhp race trim, and left them only on equal terms overall, with opposition spearheaded by Bobby Unser's still 650bhp Eagle Offenhauser.

Hill retired when his 56 lost a wheel but the remaining turbines were nevertheless well placed when one of the race's frequent yellow light periods occurred. Under the rules, drivers must slow down and may not overtake when an incident has called for the yellows, but Leonard was leading and Pollard was seventh when the green lights came on again on lap 191, just nine from the finish. As both hit their accelerator pedals again to build back up to speed their overheated turbines broke their fuel pump driveshafts, and it was 1967 all over again. Hill's car had been fitted with a special steel shaft in its fuel pump drive but United Aircraft, which had supplied the two STP entries, had insisted they continue to use the standard phosphor bronze shafts designed to fail if an engine should overheat prior to take-off when installed in a helicopter. When the turbines overheated during the

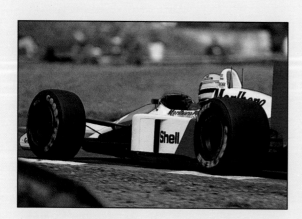

THE McLAREN MP4/4

But for a misunderstanding with a backmarker during the 1988 Italian Grand Prix, World Champion Ayrton Senna would have clinched his title sooner than the Japanese Grand Prix in October.

In the Italian race in September he was heading for victory, despite the threat from the Ferraris of Gerhard Berger and Michele Alboreto, when his McLaren MP4/4 was struck by the Williams of Frenchman Jean-Louis Schlesser, whom he was lapping.

As Senna finished his race straddling the kerb in one of Monza's slow chicanes, Honda Marlboro McLaren's remarkable string of consecutive victories was brought to a halt.

Nevertheless, the McLaren MP4/4, designed by American Steve Nichols, was the most successful Grand Prix car of the season and set a blistering tally of 15 victories from a possible 16 races. Ferrari scored seven out of seven in 1952, but that was against markedly weaker competition at a time when F1 was temporarily run to F2 rules.

Senna, too, despite that disappointment at Monza, set a new record of eight Grand Prix victories in a single season. His team-mate Alain Prost equalled his own previous record, shared with the late Jim Clark, of seven.

Ayrton Senna won a record eight Grands Prix in 1988 in the Steve Nichols-designed McLaren MP4/4. With Alain Prost winning another seven, it scored 15 successes out of a possible 16.

yellow light period, the shafts performed their fail-safe function, exactly as they were designed to . . .

Worse, immediately after the race USAC slashed the intake area again, this time to a crippling 11.999 sq in (30.477 sq cm). It was the end of the road for the turbines at Indianapolis, even though the unsuccessful Wynn's Storm Allison turbine car appeared briefly the following year. To show his displeasure, Granatelli ran his innovative cars on the complete USAC championship trail for the rest of the year, but they never won a race. As if to summarise their career, the two cars ended their last race in the wall after Mario Andretti collided with team-mate Art Pollard in the final event of the year.

In 1968 the American Howmet Corporation also ran a turbine-powered car in the World Sportscar Championship, albeit with minimal success, but that wasn't quite the end of the engine's motor racing career. Ever the daring innovator, Colin Chapman converted one of the 56s to 56B specification for Grand Prix racing in 1971, after listening to Graham Hill's favourable comments on the original 56's behaviour on American road courses.

Pratt & Whitney came up with a version of its STN/76 turbine which equated to three litres, and on wet tracks the 56B ran quite well. Emerson Fittipaldi actually qualified second for the International Trophy Race at Silverstone, but the suspension failed on the second lap of the first heat. After repairs, he was able to coax it home third in the second. In the Dutch GP Dave Walker started from the back of the grid but whooshed as high as 10th on the wet surface after only five laps. Sadly, he got over-excited and crashed underbraking for the Tarzan hairpin a lap later.

The 56B appeared in a GP for the last time at Monza that September. Lotus was still under legal threat which dated back to Jochen Rindt's death there in the original 72 the previous year, so the car appeared in black and gold colours under the auspices of World Wide Racing. The Brazilian came home an uncompetitive eighth and then took second place in a mixed Formula 5000 race at Hockenheim the following week, having started from the front row and set fastest lap. Chapman, however, knew the car was too long, too wide and too heavy for a category of racing in which agility is always paramount, and cut his losses thereafter, ending a brave experiment which proved a failure.

4WD LOSES OUT TO THE AEROFOIL

The other great blind alley of the sixties was four-wheel drive. Ferguson had used its system in a front-engined

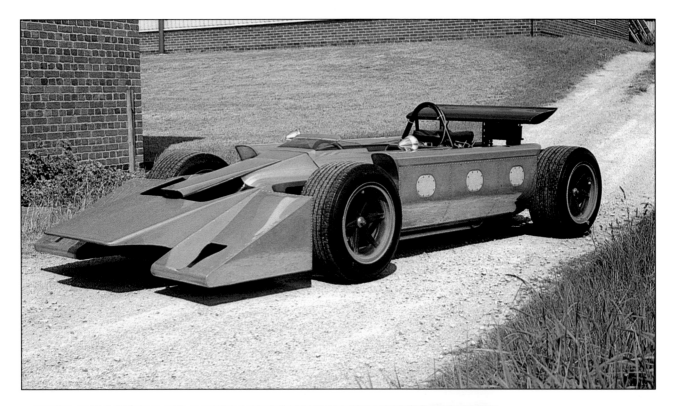

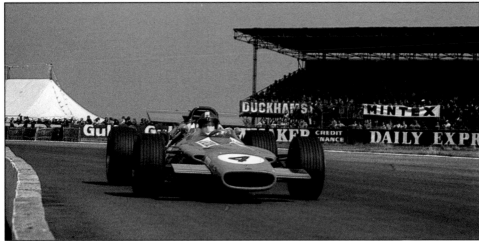

LEFT *Matra's MS84 was very similar to the title-winning MS80, in all but performance. It was the only 4WD F1 car to score a Championship point, however.*

ABOVE *Cosworth's garish 4WD F1 contender, designed by Robin Herd, never made a race after unsuccessful testing.*

machine it built in 1961, and when driven by Stirling Moss it enjoyed a modicum of success: shortly afterwards, BRM experimented with it long enough to convince itself it wasn't the way to go.

Both ventures had been based on small capacity racers, however, and when the new three-litre F1 came in for 1966, the experts predicted that it would soon be essential to harness the massive power outputs that were anticipated.

Looking back now, after the phenomenal turbo era, it is rather quaint to consider how power outputs of 150bhp per litre were deemed impressive from racing engines, but the truth is that as the new formula unfolded, anyone who could squeeze 400bhp, let alone 450, from their new three-litre engines was doing well. Racing was an awful long way off the heady days of 1985/86 when the BMW turbo four would pump out a massive 1350bhp on 5.3-bar qualifying boost – or 875bhp per litre! – and preoccupation with four-wheel drive was prevalent in 1966 even if the first fruits of designers' fresh thoughts

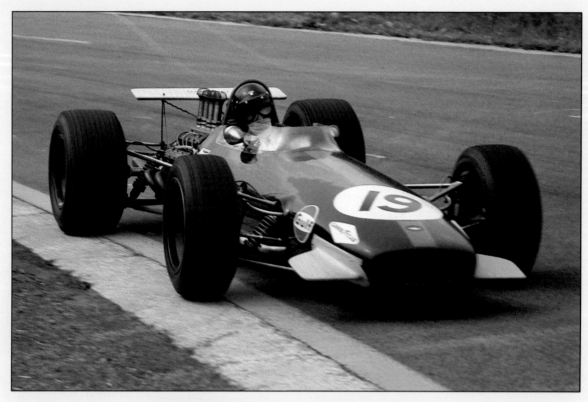

THE FIRST WINGS

The idea of using an upturned aeroplane wing – or aerofoil – to generate downforce on a racing car originated in the 1920s with the rear-engined Benz *Tropfelwagen* and the rocket-powered Opel record cars RAK 1 and 2 driven by Fritz von Opel; but the experiments were inconclusive, as was Swiss inventor Michael May's with a much larger device mounted atop his Porsche racing sports car at Monza in 1956. May abandoned his efforts but later achieved fame for his combustion chamber designs, and it wasn't until American Jim Hall revived the idea of wings in the 1960s that they began to become a mandatory feature of all serious competition machinery. In the early 1960s his fellow countryman Richie Ginther had used an upward sloping 'spoiler' to give better high-speed stability on the various sports-racing cars he drove, but now Hall used a large aerofoil mounted on high struts directly to the rear axle uprights, so that the downward pressure exerted by air flow over the wing literally forced the tyres into contact with the track. The result was markedly improved stability and cornering power, and lower lap times.

Hall's sports car racing Chaparrals won many races, and in 1965 McLaren experimented with wings on a prototype single seater with very promising results, which were then forgotten! It wasn't until the 1968 Belgian Grand Prix, however, at the very fast Spa-Francorchamps circuit that Ferrari and Brabham appeared with small, low-mounted wings on F1 cars.

The Ferraris, which arrived with wings fitted, balanced the rear-end downforce with small tabs on the nose of their 312s, while the Brabhams, whose wings appeared for the second qualifying session, had proper winglets either side of their nosecones.

Typically, it was Colin Chapman who most appreciated the value of the high strut-mounted wings, which soon appeared on his Lotus 49Bs. By 1969 similar devices were being added over the front axle, but following that year's Spanish Grand Prix, when several teams had wing failures and Lotus drivers Graham Hill and Jochen Rindt both crashed heavily as a direct result, the FIA banned the overhead aerofoils. Thereafter, wing heights, dimensions and locations have been closely regulated; but these downforce-generating devices remain a vital and integral part of modern motor racing.

LEFT *Brabham followed Ferrari's lead at Spa in 1968 by equipping its BT26s with nose fins and a low rear aerofoil.*

RIGHT *Chris Amon's high-winged Ferrari heads the field up Eau Rouge at the start of the 1968 Belgian GP at Spa, the first time a fully aero-foiled F1 car had raced.*

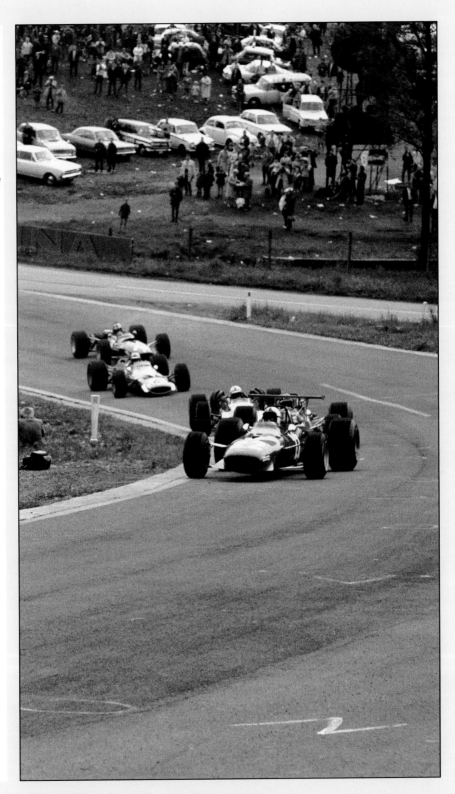

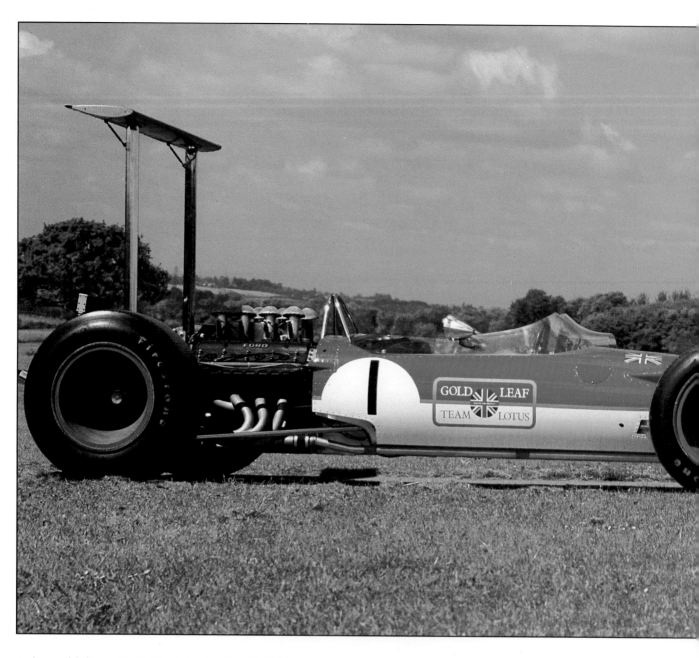

on it wouldn't see the light of day in F1 until 1969.

By then, the seeds of the system's demise had already appeared in the form of aerofoils. When Europeans' minds finally began to assimilate what American designer Jim Hall had already learned about an inverted wing's ability to load the tyres to produce significantly better grip and cornering power, F1 stood again on the verge of a revolution.

At the Belgian GP at Spa Francorchamps, Ferrari and Brabham appeared with wings. Chris Amon raced his Ferrari with one and was dicing for the lead when he retired. His team-mate Jacky Ickx didn't use one on his Ferrari, and finished third. But if there was initial scepticism, it had vanished by the end of the year. Even BRM, one of the more conservative of the established teams, had full wings by the end of the season, and the craze spread rapidly to the junior formulae as well. From that season on, single-seaters never looked the same again.

By 1969 cars sped round circuits with ungainly high wings mounted front and rear. Breakages were frequent because of the cornering loads induced, and the situation reached a head with the celebrated Lotus failures at

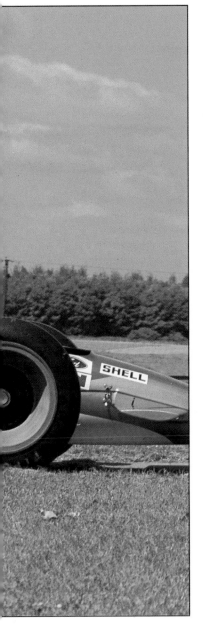

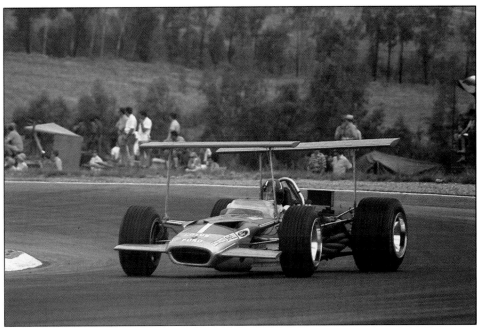

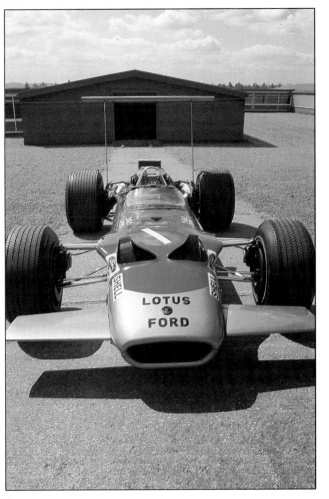

FAR LEFT Colin Chapman of
Lotus was the fastest learner
and quick to appreciate the
need for downforce over the
rear axle, rather than in the
middle of the car. He soon
equipped his 49Bs with high
rear wings.

LEFT To balance the rear
downforce, Chapman also
used wide front aerofoils to
keep the nose down. The
triangular outlets by the race
number were to allow radiator
cooling air to exit, thus also
relieving frontal lift.

ABOVE By 1969 Chapman had
added a high front wing to
supplement the nose fins, the
idea being to place the wings
as high as possible so they ran
in less turbulent air and were
thus more efficient.

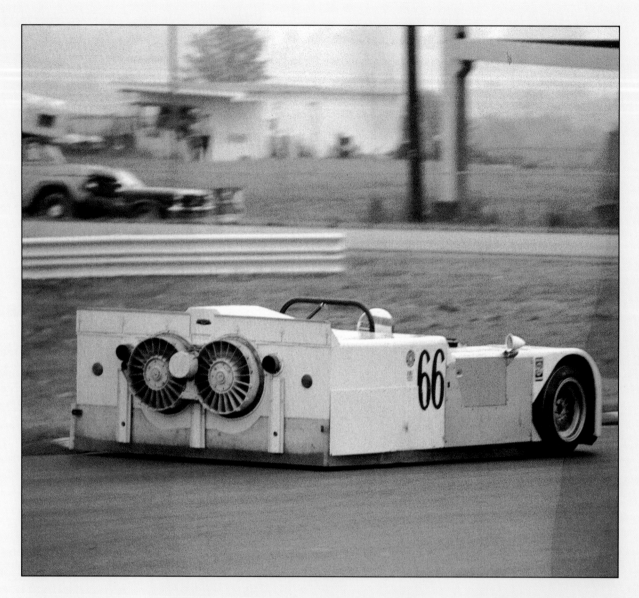

UNDER PRESSURE

One should not be surprised that it was Jim Hall who pioneered the art of harnessing under-car airflow to improve cornering grip, for the American had a talent for lateral thinking.

As his trusty Chaparral 2G began to show signs of age in the Canadian-American (Can-Am) sports car series in 1968, he worked on what was to be the unsuccessful beam-axled 2H. After that disaster, however, he bounced back with an amazing creation that looked like the sort of shape a small child might carve from a block of balsa wood.

As observers at the time joked, the 2J looked like the box it came in, but it stood the 1970 Can-Am series on its ear as it blasted the hitherto dominant McLaren M8Ds into the weeds.

Its secret was a system of plastic skirts attached to the underside of its boxy body, and a small auxiliary snowmobile two-stroke, twin-cylinder engine driving a pair of fans which literally sucked the air out from beneath the chassis to create a vacuum. With a low pressure area underneath and higher air pressure on its bodywork, its tyres were thus loaded artificially, and it was capable of awesome lap speeds that proved it to be the fastest car in the races it undertook in the hands

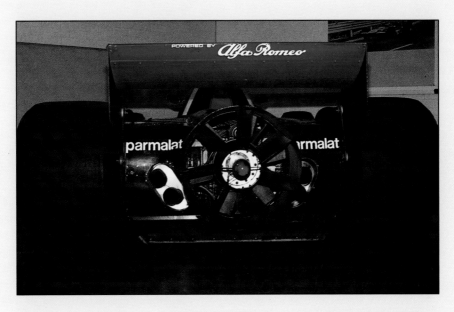

LEFT *Jim Hall's Chaparral 2J may have looked like the box it came in, but was the first car to harness ground effect, with twin rear fans sucking air from beneath it to create a ground-hugging vacuum.*

TOP RIGHT *The BT46 Fan Car emulated the Chaparral with sensational result as it won the Swedish GP. Like the 2J, it was promptly banned.*

of Jackie Stewart and Vic Elford.

It was promptly banned in America, but it set European minds thinking, as many of Hall's exploits frequently did.

In 1976 experiments at Lotus convinced Colin Chapman of the value of controlling the airflow beneath a chassis, and in his 1977 Lotus 78 he came up with a means of creating a low-pressure area beneath the car by shaping its underside into a specific form.

If air is compressed by the need to enter a restricted opening or venturi, its speed increases and its pressure drops. With lower pressure beneath the car, the higher pressure of air flowing over its bodywork helped to produce downforce, and the suction effect of the venturi completed the picture to create vastly improved grip.

Chapman progressed his ideas in the 1978 World Championship-winning Lotus 79, by incorporating longer venturis beneath the chassis, and the car's one real scare in a year in which it dominated, came when Brabham raced its 'fan car' in Sweden.

Team owner Bernie Ecclestone hit on the idea of using a cooling fan on the flat-12 Alfa Romeo engine and getting it to perform a double function of sucking the air from beneath the car. Although the engine-driven fan cost some power, the road-holding was so fantastic that the BT46 wiped the floor even with the Lotus as Niki Lauda won as he pleased. Within a week, that car too was banned . . .

Ground effect itself progressed to sliding skirts to cater for differences in the road surface while preventing air being sucked into the venturi area from either side of the car and thus reducing the level of adhesion.

Colin Chapman further refined his original concept by producing the Lotus 88, which had one chassis which acted as a giant wing to create downforce and another which cocooned the driver and spared him from the usual spine-jarring ride associated with ground-effect racers. It, too, was banned, without ever having raced.

Shaped undersides were also banned from F1 cars in 1983, but astute interpretation of the regulations still permits the current breed of flat-bottomed cars to develop significant downforce by careful management of airflow beneath their chassis.

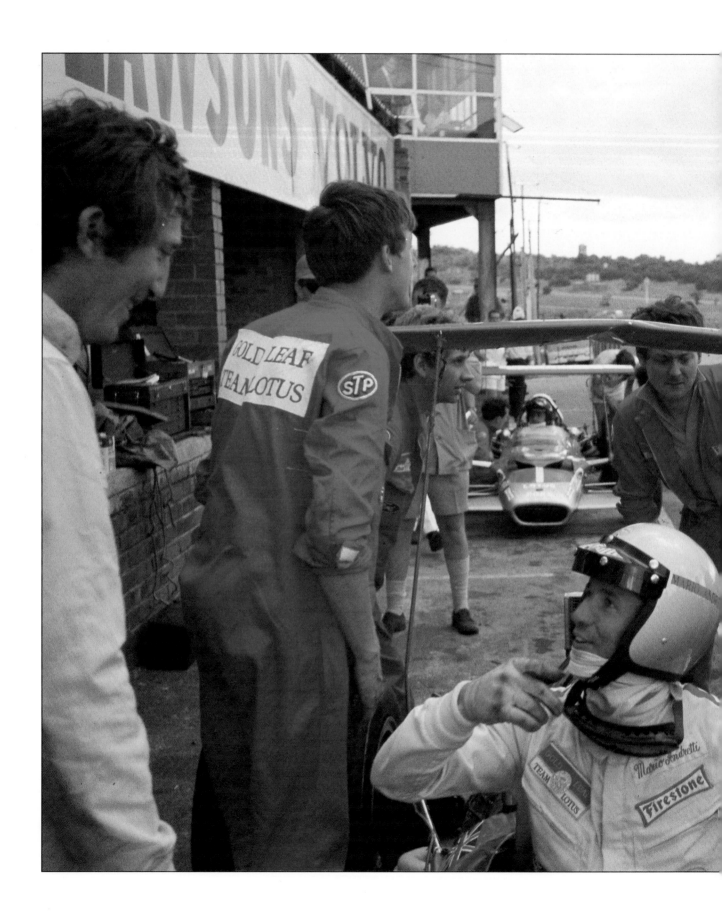

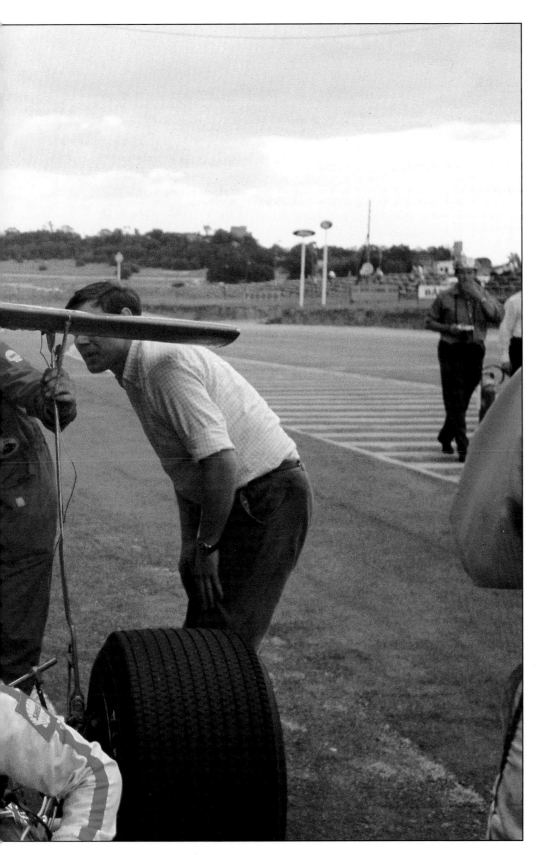

'The handling's gone away'.
Mario Andretti and team-mate
Jochen Rindt joke about the
former's rear wing failure
during practice for the 1969
South African GP at Kyalami.
Months later similar failures
weren't so funny as they put
Rindt and Graham Hill out of
the Spanish GP, and led to a
ban on high-mounted
aerofoils.

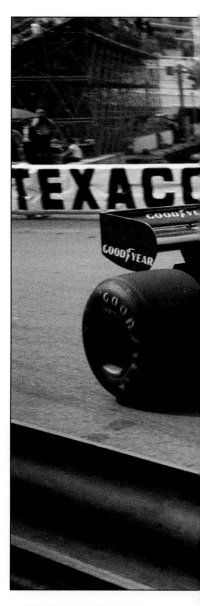

RIGHT *Tyrrell's 1976 P34 had more than just novelty value. The innovative six-wheeler was a consistent finisher in the top three, and took Jody Scheckter to victory in Sweden ahead of team-mate Patrick Depailler. The idea was to reduce frontal area with four small wheels rather than two larger, but the concept eventually foundered when Goodyear had to concentrate its development on conventional tyres for the Tyrrell's rivals.*

Montjuich Park in Barcelona. By the following race wing heights were truncated, and cornering force was temporarily reduced. The stage finally seemed set for four-wheel drive.

Lotus and Matra certainly thought so, as Colin Chapman worked on the Lotus 63 and Derek Gardner on the Matra MS84, while McLaren also experimented and so did Cosworth, although the engine manufacturer's own F1 car was never actually to race.

The Lotus, typically, was an all-new car which drew heavily on Chapman's experience with the Indianapolis turbine cars, while the Matra was literally a 4WD version of the MS80 that would take Jackie Stewart to that year's world crown.

All of the cars were to prove a total failure. In theory, the advantage of being able to put more power on the road should have been decisive. After all, 4WD had worked fine at Indianapolis, and elsewhere on the USAC trail. But on the road circuits used in F1, it gave no discernible advantage, even in the wet, where much had been expected of its superior traction. The systems used were too heavy, there was excessive weight bias to the rear of the cars, which created insurmountable understeer, and the cars were simply too unwieldy.

Jochen Rindt and Graham Hill declined to drive the Lotus 63s in GPs, although John Miles did take one to ninth at Silverstone and Rindt was a poor second in a non-championship event at Oulton Park. By season end the Matra had 90% of its power going to the rear wheels, which rather defeated the object, and was still uncompetitive, while the McLaren M9A raced only once and was pushed away.

Advances in F1 tyre design (brought about by the war between Dunlop, Firestone and Goodyear), and the development of wings, had resulted in dramatically increased cornering forces without any weight penalty. In an environment as competitive as F1, there simply wasn't the time to develop new concepts that didn't offer an advantage immediately, and 4WD was quietly dropped. Those who had predicted it would be essential to cope with the expected 500bhp outputs were proved wrong as 2WD proved perfectly adequate for 1350bhp: but 4WD would still have its competition day (see Chapter Four).

In 1981 it seemed it might have a brief stay of execution when Williams produced a 4WD version of its successful FW07C, but this was in fact a six-wheeler wherein an extra rear axle had been grafted on to reduce the size of the rear tyre diameters and enhance traction and aero-

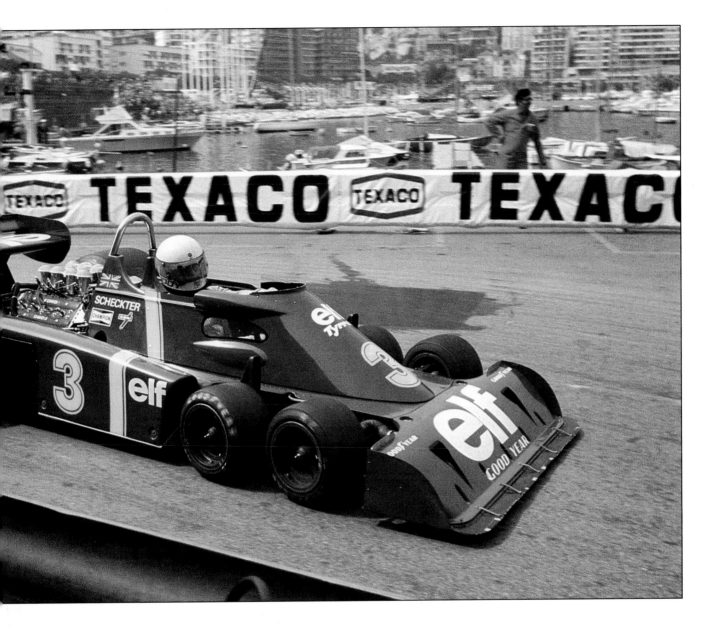

dyamics. The 1982 World Champion Keke Rosberg tested it at the Paul Ricard circuit in France, but the idea never progressed. Like March, which had tried a similar experiment on a 761 chassis in the mid-seventies, Williams met with trouble integrating the two axles.

The six-wheel theme had also been tried, with greater success, by Tyrrell. In late 1975 Derek Gardner produced the P34, which used four tiny front wheels to reduce frontal area and enhance turn-in grip. The concept was sufficiently impressive to merit building racing versions, which Tyrrell used for two seasons.

Jody Scheckter became the only man to win a Grand Prix in a six-wheeled car when he led team-mate Patrick Depailler home in the 1976 Swedish GP, and altogether the cars were second seven times that year. They were modified for 1977 but there was less development on their unique front tyres and they were less competitive. Besides which, a new phenomenon had hit motor racing.

GROUND EFFECT

Again, it was Chapman who had created the concept that was to change the face of racing once more, as his staff under Ralph Bellamy and Peter Wright began successfully to control airflow beneath the car to enhance roadholding.

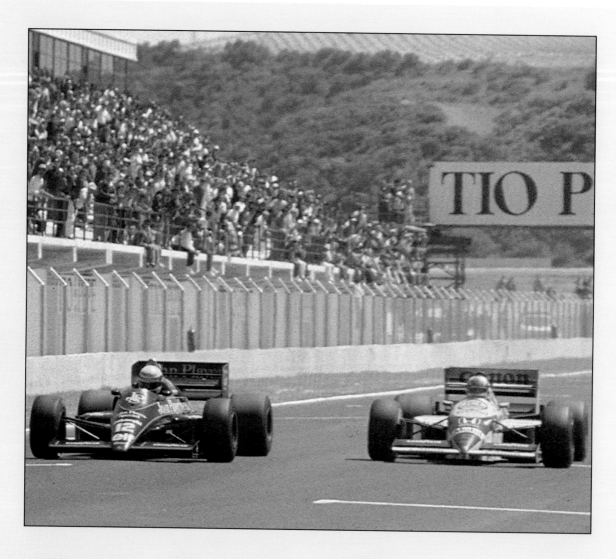

CLOSEST FINISHES

The closest finish ever officially recorded in a Grand Prix came in 1986, when the Spanish Grand Prix was held for the first time at the new Jerez circuit.

Briton Nigel Mansell had led in his Canon Williams-Honda FW11 but dropped behind Ayrton Senna in his JPS Lotus-Renault 98T after a pit stop for new tyres. Round the twisting track he closed rapidly on the Brazilian in the final laps, and was on his tail as they swept to the line at the end of the 188 mile (302km), 72-lap race. Senna clung on to take the verdict by 0.014 seconds. Had the finish line not been moved closer to the last corner prior to the race, Mansell would have been the winner . . .

In the Austrian GP of 1982, once the faster turbo cars had run themselves into the ground, Elio De Angelis and Keke Rosberg were left fighting their normally-aspirated way to the line in Lotus 91 and Williams FW08 respectively. Though the Finn tried a desperate slipstreaming sweep round the final corner, the Italian led him over the line by a scant 0.050 seconds.

At the 1969 Italian Grand Prix the first *four* cars were covered by 0.44 seconds as

ABOVE *How close is close? At Jerez in the 1986 Spanish GP, Ayrton Senna (left) just pips Nigel Mansell to victory. The official margin was 0.014 seconds!*

ABOVE RIGHT *On the last corner of the 1969 Italian GP at Monza, Jean-Pierre Beltoise dives inside team-mate Jackie Stewart, as Jochen Rindt and Bruce McLaren give chase. Stewart won from Rindt, Beltoise and McLaren, with a mere 0.44 seconds covering all four.*

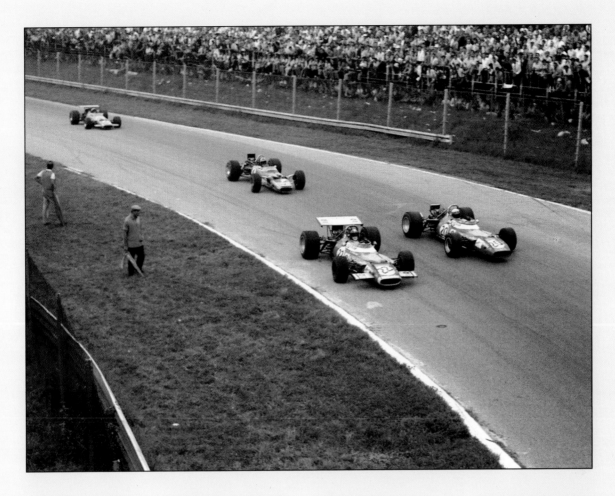

Jackie Stewart (Matra MS80), Jochen Rindt (Lotus 49B, −0.080s), Bruce McLaren (McLaren M7B, −0.17s) and Jean-Pierre Beltoise (Matra, −0.19s) dashed to the finish line in that order after a high-speed slipstreaming epic.

Two years later, Briton Peter Gethin scored the only Grand Prix win of his career at the same venue when his Yardley BRM P160 led Ronnie Peterson's March 711, Francois Cevert's Tyrrell 002, Mike Hailwood's Surtees TS9 and Howden Ganley's Yardley BRM P160 under the chequered flag with only 0.89 seconds separating them all! The governing bodies have always frowned on contrived dead heat finishes. In the 1967 non-championship Syracuse Grand Prix, Mike Parkes and Ludovico Scarfiotti crossed the line side by side in their Ferrari 312s, while a year earlier Ford had tried to stage a dead heat when it realized it was going to win its first Le Mans 24 Hours. It slowed the leading MkII driven by Denny Hulme and Ken Miles and matched it exactly with the similar car driven by Chris Amon and Bruce McLaren. However, the plan backfired on Hulme and Miles, who had led convincingly. They had qualified second and thus started higher up the line than McLaren and Amon, who qualified 0.9 seconds slower in fourth place. The FIA ruled that the Amon/McLaren car was the official victor since it had covered more ground in the 24 hours, having started further back. Messrs Hulme and Miles were not amused, since they had effectively been penalized for qualifying at a higher speed; had Miles not allowed McLaren to draw alongside on the finish line, he and Hulme would have won!

Three years later Jackie Ickx and Hans Herrmann produced the closest genuine finish ever seen in the sports car classic, when they duelled for the final three hours in Ford GT40 and Porsche 908 respectively and crossed the line only 20 metres apart after 3,105 miles (4,955km).

RIGHT *Stripped of its bodywork, John Barnard's McLaren MP4/1 reveals its black carbon fibre structure. This innovative use of composite materials resulted in an incredibly strong machine and sparked off a revolution in racing car design technology.*

OPPOSITE *The 1981 Lotus 88, seen in Nigel Mansell's hands during qualifying for the British GP at Silverstone, was another innovative attempt to reconcile the need for stiff suspension and ground effect with driver comfort. As usual, it was the product of Colin Chapman's fertile ability to think laterally, but he never got over its exclusion by the governing body.*

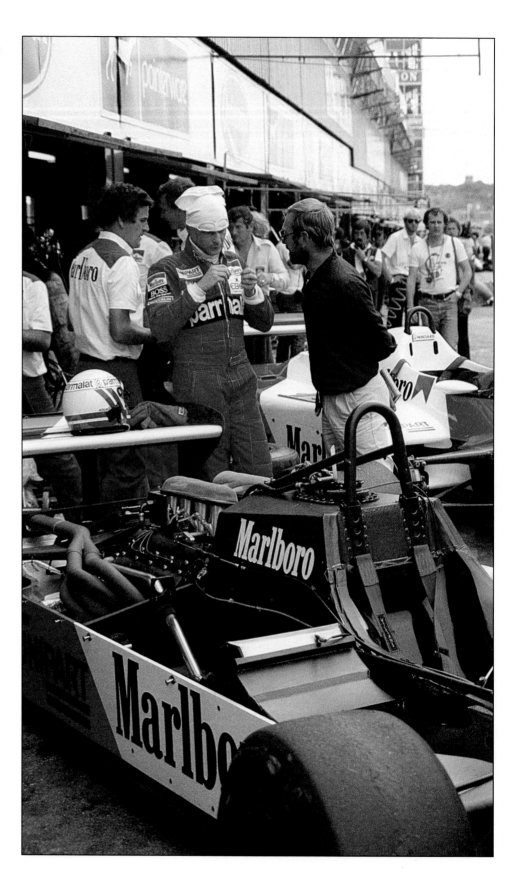

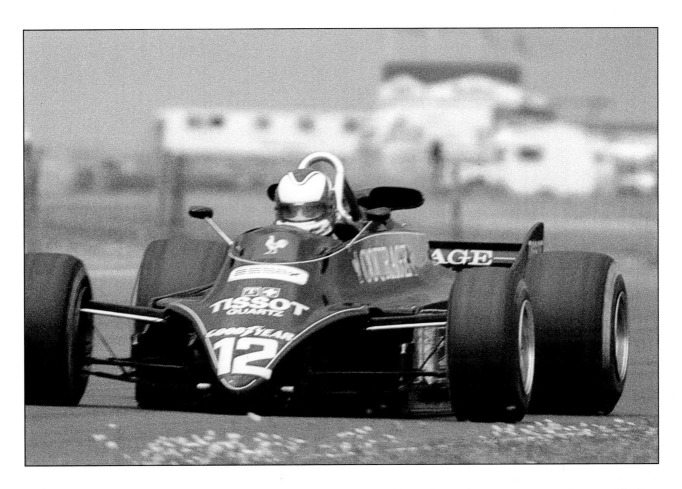

Through 1977 the Lotus 78 rewrote the record books on handling, and only lack of reliability and a little driver over-enthusiasm kept the American Mario Andretti from the world title. He took it in style the following year in the developed 79, which had full under-car venturis and sited the driver further forward in the chassis, ahead of a giant central fuel cell.

The speed of the Lotus initiated a rush of ground-effect development. Initially, the side skirts that prevented air spilling in from the outside, and thus reducing the suction effect, were rigid. Then Patrick Head at Williams hit on a method of making them slide vertically, so that the car remained more stable over bumpy surfaces. To minimize movement, the suspension travel was limited, to the point where the cars became twitchy, a nervousness that punished their drivers. But they were breathtakingly fast as they generated cornering forces up to 4G, and following that dangerous route became the only way to win. Yet again, Chapman thought up a novel means of having his ground effect cake and eating it without pummeling the driver, with his twin-chassis 88 in

1981. This used one chassis to generate the ground effect, and another in which to insulate the driver. The governing body FISA had several looks at it before deciding it contravened the regulations, and one of the most innovative answers to the problem of driver comfort and safety passed into history.

Today, the new breed of normally aspirated cars is generating nearly 4G in corners thanks to further aerodynamic and tyre developments, the suspension movement is still as little as 10mm (0.03in), and the drivers are still pounded, which proves that, in motor racing, what goes around tends to come around.

Had ground effect been allowed to continue, one can only speculate on the cornering speeds modern F1 cars might generate, but it was banned by FISA from the 1983 season onwards. Shaped undersides were no longer permitted between a car's front and rear axle lines, but a flick-up at the rear was still allowed, and if the front of a car could be run low enough to create a low pressure area beneath the chassis, this diffusor could still help it generate a healthy amount of downforce.

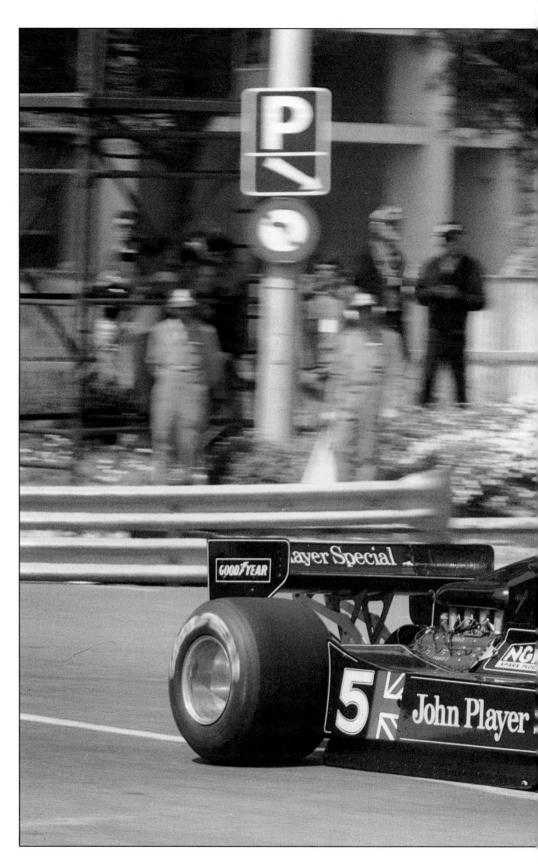

At Monaco in 1978, that season's World Champion Mario Andretti makes full use of the Lotus 78's super-precise turn-in at the Portier corner. The 78 was the first F1 design successfully to exploit undercar aerodynamics to promote ground effect, and started a revolution.

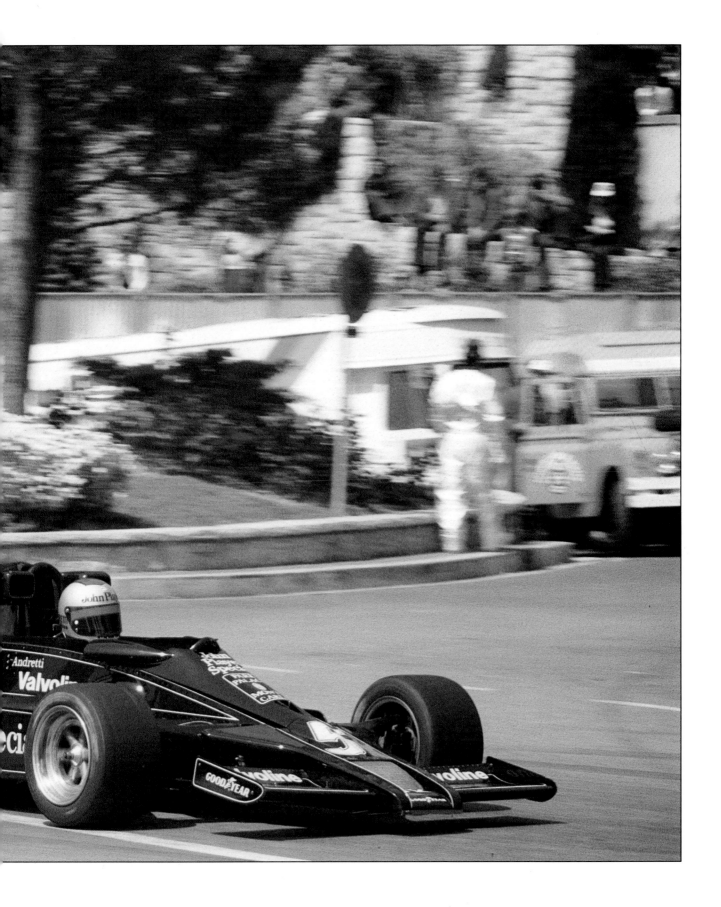

CONSTRUCTIONAL METHODS AND MATERIALS

Part of Colin Chapman's genius was not only to come up with fresh ideas, but to implement existing ones successfully. Prior to 1962 racing car chassis were built as spaceframes of welded steel or aluminium tubes. They were simple to make but lacked strength and torsional rigidity. Using aircraft principles, Chapman devised a method of unitary construction in which the chassis comprised a series of aluminium bulkheads linked by aluminium torsion boxes to form a monocoque or one-piece structure. It was stiffer, stronger and lighter and within years became the standard method of construction.

Jim Hall of Chaparral fame took the theory further by producing monocoques for his sports cars made out of glass reinforced fibre (GRP), and in 1966 Robin Herd's McLaren M2B F1 car used a special honeycomb of aluminium sandwiching a layer of balsa wood, while Ford's Le Mans J car that year, and its 1967 Le Mans-winning MkIV, used sheets of aluminium which sandwiched a honeycomb of the same material. Honeycomb is lighter and stiffer than conventional aluminium, and by the latter half of the 1970s had become the new standard F1 car material.

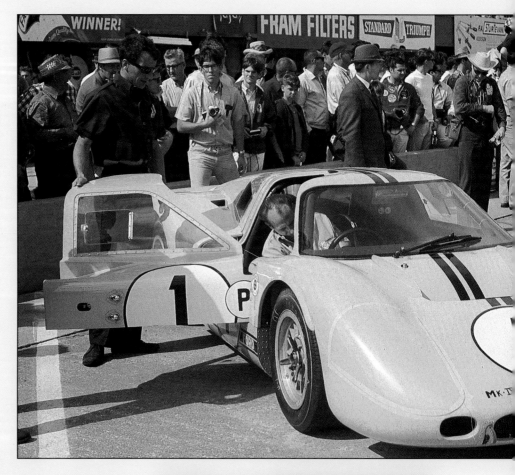

Honeycomb had come from the aircraft industry, and so did what was to become the next new material: carbon fibre. English designer John Barnard was the first to harness the properties of this remarkable material when he produced what became the McLaren MP4/1 for the 1981 season. The panels were bonded together and then baked in a giant oven called an autoclave, and the result was a chassis that was phenomenally strong yet even lighter than a conventional honeycomb aluminium counterpart.

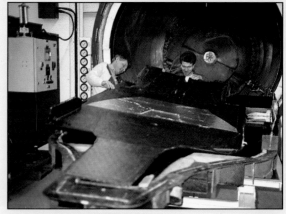

Carbon fibre composite chassis have developed rapidly, using additional layers of material such as Kevlar or Nomex, and by the end of the 1980s had become standard for F1 cars and increasingly popular as a chassis material in many other racing categories.

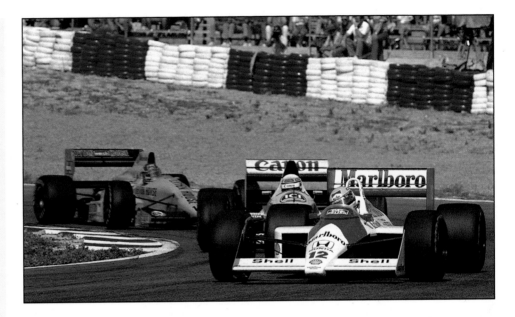

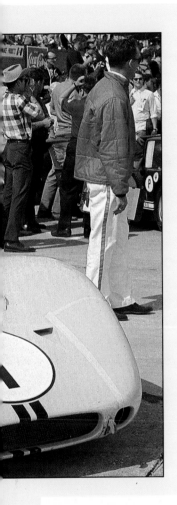

LEFT *Designer Harvey Postlethwaite (left) supervises removal of a carbon fibre composite undertray for the 1989 Tyrrell 018 from the giant autoclave (oven) in which it has been baked. The autoclave, like the wind tunnel, is now an essential part of any serious F1 team's armoury.*

ABOVE *The 1967 Ford MkIV sportscar was one of the first to utilize honeycomb aluminium in its structure, following tests on the prototype J car the previous year. It won here at Sebring, and again later at Le Mans.*

The rule change achieved its desired effect in 1983 of slowing the cars, but coincided with rapid development of turbocharged engines. They had come into F1 with Renault in 1977 and had developed steadily until engineers turned their attention to electronic engine management systems in 1983. From 580bhp, power outputs began to climb over 650bhp, and as the management systems allowed more precise monitoring and governing of ignition timing and fuel injection, boost pressures and compression ratios climbed too and a power race was well and truly on. By 1986, even though FISA progressively tried to restrict power outputs by limiting the amount of fuel cars could carry during a race, Honda's V6 developed 1100bhp on 4.3-bar boost (4.3 times normal atmospheric pressure, which is 14.7psi), while the four-cylinder BMW had a staggering 1350 on 5.3-bar for short spells!

As a telling indication of the rate of progress in F1, the new non-turbo cars are just as fast now with only 600–650bhp, and part of that is explained by advances in constructional materials. The appearance of the carbon fibre composite McLaren MP4/1 coincided with the point at which turbo advances boosted power outputs and aerodynamic developments created greater and greater forces upon the cars. The stiffness and inherent strength of the carbon composite chassis came at a time when such qualities were sorely needed, and such developments now march hand-in-hand with further electronic advances as the latest atmospheric cars take racing into a new era.

ABOVE *By 1988 technology had advanced to the point where the turbocharged F1 cars such as Ayrton Senna's McLaren MP4/4 (seen here leading Riccardo Patrese's non-turbo Williams and Ivan Capelli's non-turbo March) were every bit as fast with only 2.5-bar boost as their 4-bar counterparts had been the previous season.*

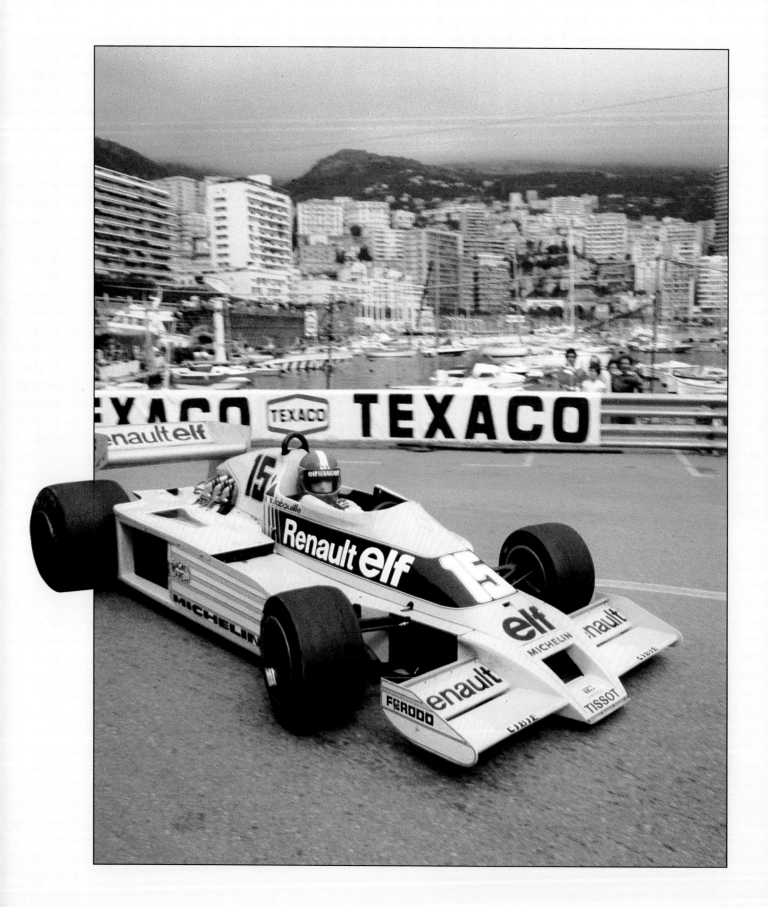

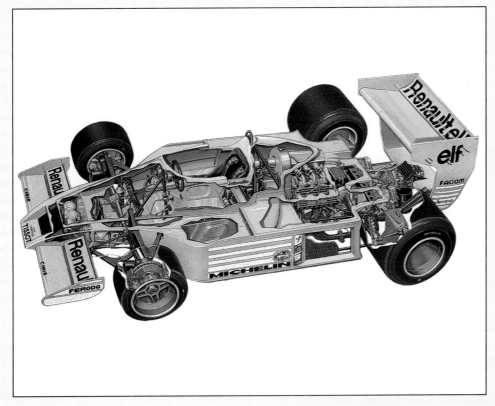

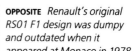

OPPOSITE *Renault's original RS01 F1 design was dumpy and outdated when it appeared at Monaco in 1978, and its throttle lag made it a nightmare to drive round the steel-lined circuit.*

LEFT *As this cutaway reveals, it made precious little use of ground effect and was basically a development of the F2-based prototype with which most of the team's pre-racing testing had been conducted in 1977.*

BELOW LEFT *The RE30B introduced for 1981 was a much more serious proposition that performed well enough to lead even at Monaco in 1982. Only appalling reliability prevented it winning the World Championship.*

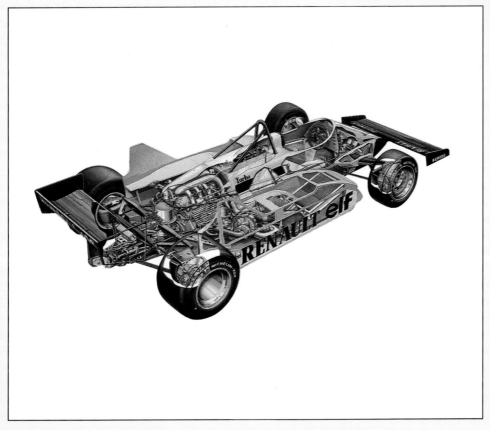

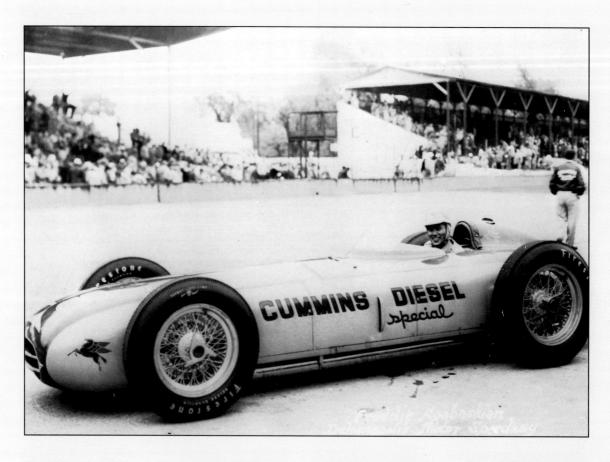

THE FIRST TURBOS

Until the 1950s, the accepted method of boosting an engine's power was to supercharge it, by forcing it into the intakes instead of relying purely on the suction effect created as the pistons rotated. The super-charger comprised a crankshaft-driven rotor which compressed air and then fed it directly into the cylinders. Forced to breathe more air and fuel mixture, the engine produced greater power. The disadvantage was that some of that extra power was taken up driving the rotor.

After World War II a new device called a turbo-charger began to appear, initially on aircraft, tractors and trucks. It used the engine's exhaust gases to drive a large impeller turbine mounted within a casing, and mixed them with air drawn in through the normal intake. The compressed mixture was then fed into the cylinders to boost the power. The great advantage of the turbine was that it didn't require any power to drive it, since it used the engine's wastes anyway, but whenever the driver backed off it took a while for the turbine to work back up to speed when he

depressed the throttle pedal again. This throttle lag – it was as much as five seconds in early installations – was to prove its greatest bugbear.

The first racing application of the new component came at Indianapolis in 1952. A change in engine rules in 1950 had encouraged the Cummins Engine Company into racing, and though its first supercharged effort failed, it returned in 1952 with a turbocharged diesel unit that boasted a competitive 400bhp at 4,000rpm on 20psi boost. Installed in a sensationally low chassis produced by

renowned builder Frank Kurtis, it staggered the opposition. Driver Freddie Agabashian lapped the red and yellow Cummins Diesel Special at a four-lap average of 139.10mph (223.81kmh) to start from pole position, despite the alarming throttle lag. Sadly, the low position of its frontal turbocharger air intake worked against it in the 500-mile (804km) race. After 175 miles (280km) the intake had sucked up rubber and track debris and clogged, and the innovative racer was retired. Rather typically, the establishment then legislated the diesel engine capacity downwards to keep the petrol counterparts in with a chance, and Cummins withdrew for good.

Twenty-three years later, no doubt having noted the success of subsequent turbo engines at Indianapolis, Renault began experimenting with turbocharging on its 2-litre sports car engine, and won the opening round of the 1975 sports car championship at Mugello with it. Thus encouraged, it gave the go-ahead for a 1.5-litre version to exploit the hitherto ignored clause in the F1 regulations that allowed three-litre normally-aspirated engines or forced induction units of half that capacity.

When the Renault RS01 F1 car appeared at the British GP at Silverstone in 1977 it made a poor debut, retiring from a lowly position with a cracked inlet manifold. The F1 world laughed.

It stopped laughing at the French GP two years later when the Renault turbo scored an historic win, and by 1981 Ferrari, Hart and BMW were experimenting with similar engines. By 1983 every team needed a turbo to be competitive and from that season until turbos were finally banned at the end of 1988, the normally-aspirated engine was completely eclipsed.

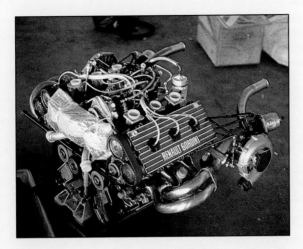

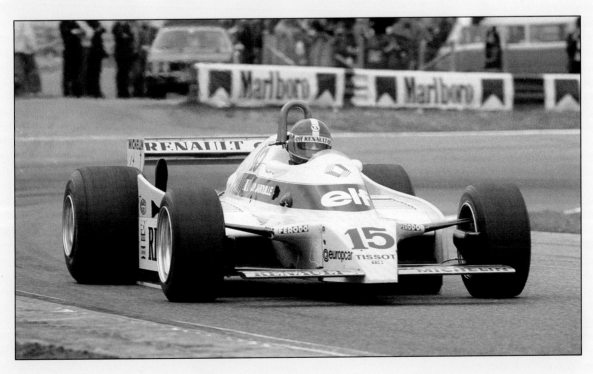

OPPOSITE *The 1952 Cummins Diesel Special was the first turbo-charged race car, and qualified for the Indy 500 pole in Freddy Agabashian's hands.*

LEFT *Although Renault's V6 was considered a joke when the Regie introduced the turbo to F1 in 1977, it was generally rated the best engine in the formula in its final season in 1986.*

BELOW *At Dijon in 1979 Jean-Pierre Jabouille heads for an historic first win for the turbo Renault.*

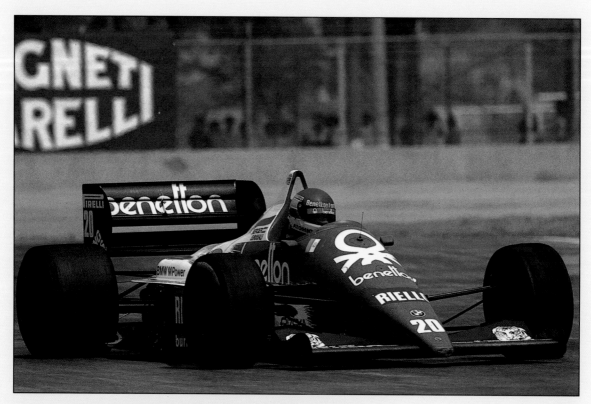

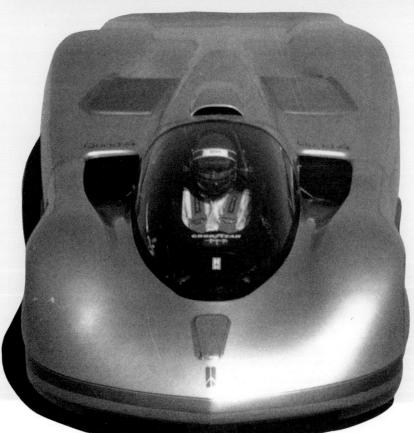

ABOVE Probably the most powerful turbocar ever was the 1350bhp Benetton-BMW B186, with which Gerhard Berger won the 1986 Mexican GP.

LEFT Legendary American Indy and sprint car racer A. J. Foyt used this March-built Oldsmobile Aerotech to achieve a new closed course record of 257.123mph at a private test track in Arizona in August 1987. He was 52 years old at the time.

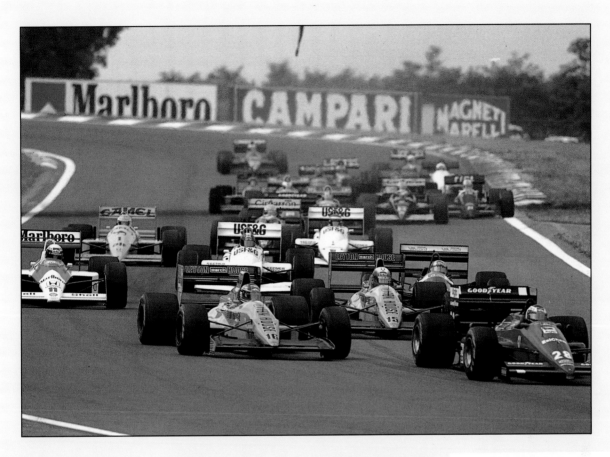

CLOSED COURSE RECORDS

Speed over a wide, open salt flat is one thing, but closed race courses present a completely different set of problems. In August 1987 Indianapolis legend Anthony Joseph (A.J.) Foyt lapped a test track in Arizona at 257.123mph (413.710kmh) in his Oldsmobile Quad 4-engined Aerotech, to obliterate Rick Mears' record of 233.934mph (376.399kmh) set in a Penske March 86C at the Michigan International Speedway in 1986. That in itself had beaten Mark Donohue's 1975 mark of 221.160mph (355.846kmh) set at Talladega Speedway in a Porsche 917/30.
By 1989, despite frequent changes in the regulations to slow the cars, CART (Championship Auto Racing Teams) single-seaters were lapping the American oval speedways at speeds over 220mph (354kmh) during practice for races.
In 1985, during qualifying for the British GP, Finn Keke Rosberg lapped the Silverstone GP circuit in Northamptonshire, England in 1 minute 5.591 seconds in his Williams-Honda FW10, an average speed of 160.925mph (258.928kmh). It was the first – and so far the only – 160mph (257kmh) lap in F1.
In 1973, at the Spa-Francorchamps road circuit in the Haute Fagnes region of Belgium, Frenchman Henri Pescarolo lapped his 3-litre Matra MS670 in 3 minutes 13.4 seconds at an average speed of 163.093mph. That stands as an all-time record for a European circuit, as Spa has since been shortened.

ABOVE *In 1988 the turbocharged cars had been limited to 2.5-bar boost, which put most of them on a par with their 3.5-litre normally aspirated rivals. Here in Hungary Berger's turbo Ferrari leads the atmo Marches of Capelli and Gugelmin, Prost's turbo McLaren, Caffi's atmo Dallara and the turbo Arrows of Warwick and Cheever, which sandwich Piquet's turbo Lotus.*

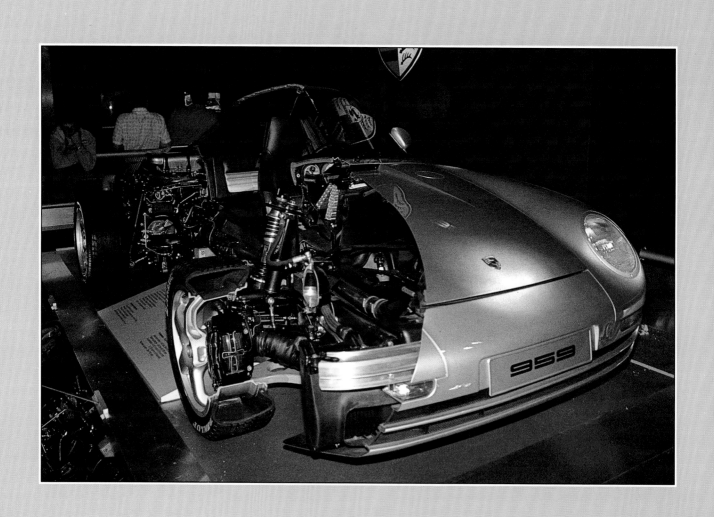

CHAPTER FOUR

WINNING ON THE ROAD

Major Developments in Production Cars

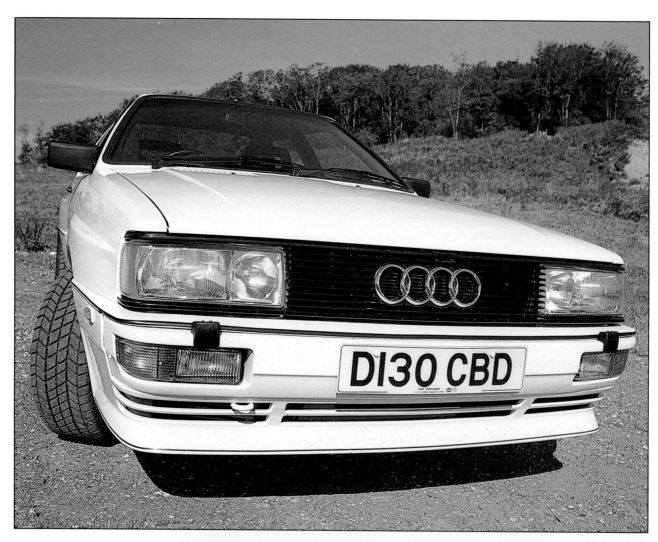

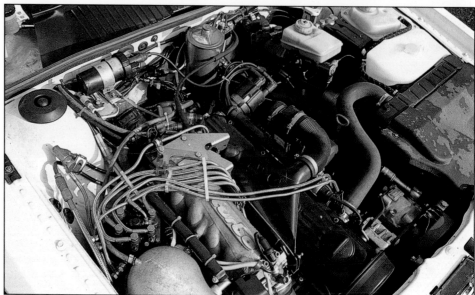

ABOVE *The spirit of the thoroughbred road car was never better illustrated than by Audi's Quattro. It was introduced in 1980 after engineer Ferdinand Piech had convinced the company's board of its merit by equipping a saloon with his 4WD system and then driving it up a slippery grass slope no other Audi vehicle could negotiate.*

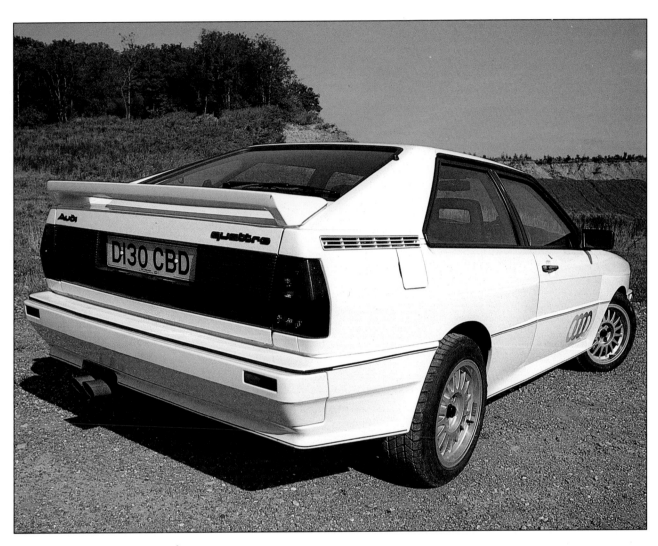

LEFT *The 2.2-litre engine featured fuel injection and five cylinders. In rally guise it made the Quattro easily the most powerful car of its day, and the 4WD allowed the driver to exploit its potential to the full.*

It is often suggested that motor racing improves the breed. To some extent that has been true – witness the development of disc brakes, for example – and there is no doubt that a manufacturer learns a great deal more about his products, and learns a great deal *faster*, in the crucible of competition.

Now, especially at the higher, more esoteric, levels such as Grand Prix racing, the benefits are less easy to quantify. In recent years there have even been grounds to suggest that developments in road car technology have been of benefit to the sport. Racing, nevertheless, continues to spawn fresh technology that may eventually benefit the man in the street. It is true that motorsport has become more and more a marketing tool, particularly since commercial advertising was allowed in Europe from 1968, but at its leading edge are the best automotive designers in the world.

ABOVE *The Quattro proved that, in both road and rally applications, 4WD could be a thoroughly practical and successful proposition. Its system might not have been the most sophisticated, but it was certainly highly effective.*

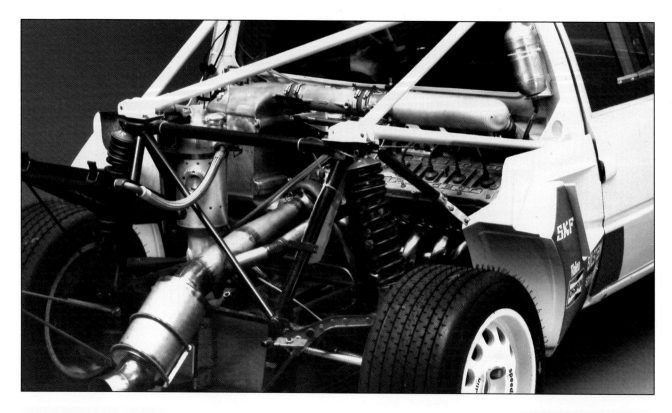

ABOVE *Peugeot's 205 T16 was probably the best rally car of all time, and was certainly run by one of the best teams. Its 1775cc four cylinder engine was mounted transversely behind the cockpit and, turbocharged at 2- to 3-bar, produced a minimum 450bhp. In Group B guise it was closer to 500, and for the famous Pike's Peak mountain climb in the US figures of 700bhp were not unknown.*

Their influence may not always be obvious in terms of potential future roadcar benefits, but it is there nonetheless. The turbocharged era of Grand Prix racing presaged a wave of turbocharged variants of production saloons and coupés, and the post-1983 advances in engine management systems have had a massive influence on everyday motoring as the exigencies of fuel economy and low pollution levels have been satiated.

Making electronics survive in as hostile an environment as a racing car is undoubtedly a useful exercise. So too is development of new compound mixing and carcass construction technniques in racing tyres, particularly now that the majority of senior formulae run on radial ply tyres. Nobody is pretending that road and racing tyres have much in common, but the lessons learned by participating companies like Goodyear, Pirelli and Bridgestone can have direct production spin-offs. They *have* to, given the boardroom pressure to justify the vast cost of a racing programme in more than just advertising terms.

Although, as we have seen, four-wheel drive (4WD) failed to make it first time around in motorsport, the 1980 Audi Quattro went a long way towards salvaging the concept. Designed by Ferdinand Piech, the rugged five-cylinder, 2,144cc machine transmitted its 200bhp through all four wheels. The 1966 Jensen FF, with its

FAR RIGHT, TOP *The original T16 E1 became the car others sought to emulate. Peugeot sold 200 road versions, but they were relatively 'slow', on a par with the British club rallyman's favourite, the Lotus Sunbeam.*

ABOVE RIGHT *The E2, or Evolution 2, version was necessary to stem the tide of increased opposition, and carried further aerodynamic aids such as the chin and roof spoilers.*

RIGHT *The 205 T16 was the first mid-engined rally car and the most successful, winning the World Rally Championship in the four seasons in which it was eligible to compete.*

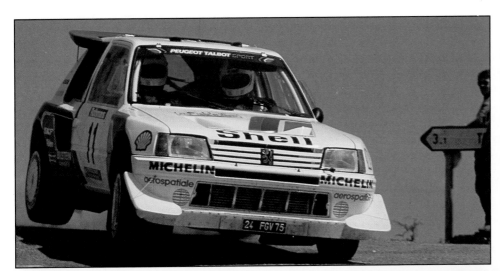

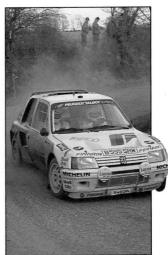

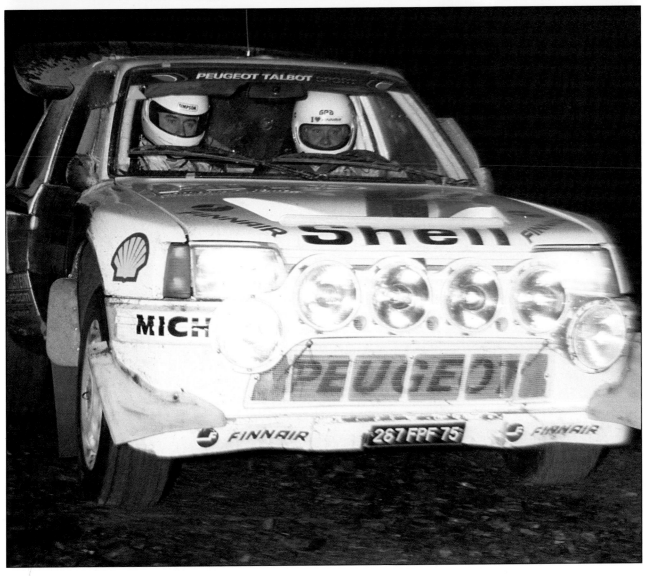

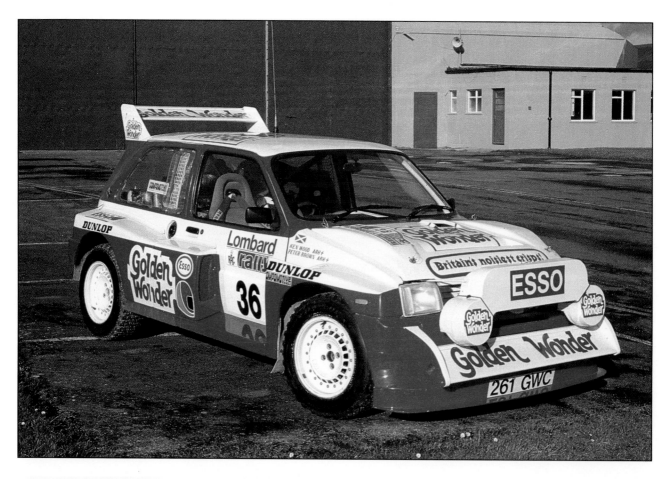

ABOVE *The MG Metro 6R4 simply arrived on the scene too late, and never really worked in the manner intended. Using a non-turbo engine was a gamble that might well have paid off had the car appeared two seasons earlier than it did, as it was faster than the original Quattros and T16s. Though it lacked development, it was nonetheless the ideal car for the rally privateer in the late Eighties.*

Ferguson Formula system, had been the first 4WD production car, but the Quattro was the first *volume* production car, and was to open the floodgates once Hannu Mikkola had driven it to a stunning victory in the 1981 Swedish Rally. Peugeot introduced its 205 T16 rally car in 1983, and it was followed by Lancia's Delta S4 in 1985 and the Ford RS200 and MG Metro 6R4 a year later. Within that five-year span 4WD went from being a competition joke to a serious technical avenue, and the effect in production car terms was stronger still. The Audi set spectacular standards for road behaviour, and thanks to the development of Ferguson's Viscous Coupling which reduced the amount of power absorbed by the transmission, 4WD became a desirable feature for road cars.

Like turbos, 4WD upmarket derivatives marked out the manufacturer with his finger on the pulse. The system's inherent characteristics of traction advantage and enhanced safety, allied to the lower weight conferred by modern manufacturing techniques, yield significant long-term benefits which should ensure that 4WD is more than a passing fad.

OPPOSITE *Lancia's Delta S4 was constructed along similar lines to the sports-racing Ferraris of the Sixties, with a steel spaceframe chassis wrapped in stressed skin. It was the most complex of all rally cars, using a supercharger and a turbocharger. The former reduced throttle lag normally associated with turbos, and a coupling disconnected its drive at a pre-selected stage, whereupon the turbo took over. The S4 was never quite as good as the Peugeot, and though it won in Europe, it became the only Lancia rally car never to win the World Rally Championship. It was, however, the source of technical inspiration for the road-going Integrale model.*

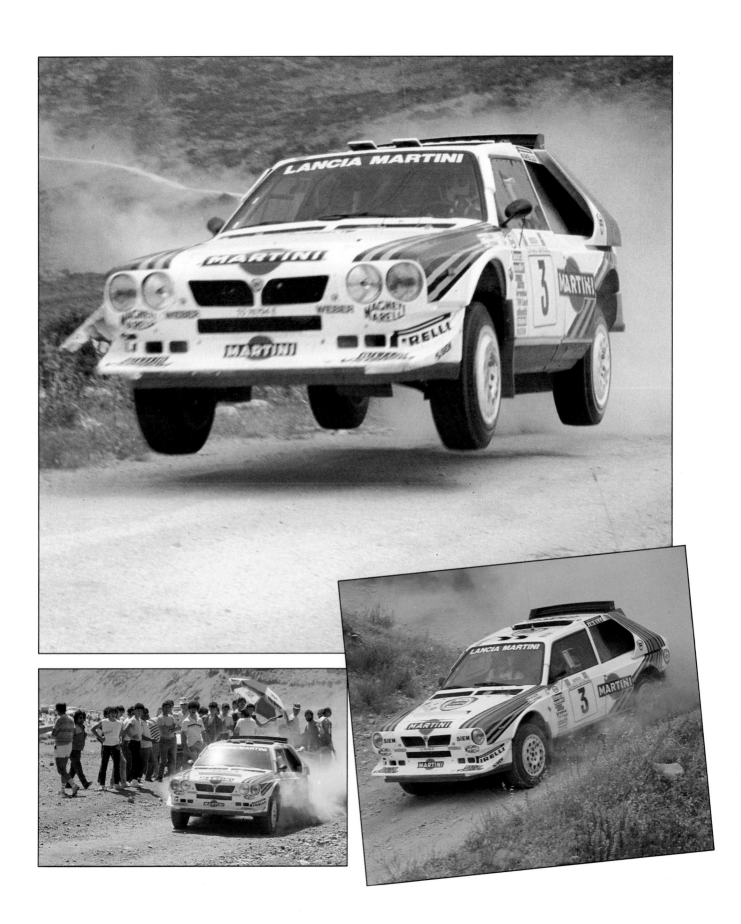

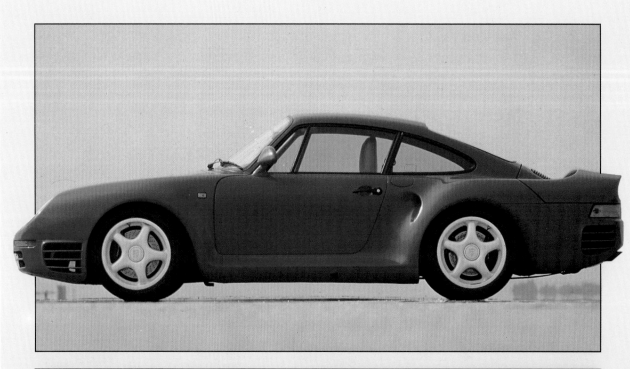

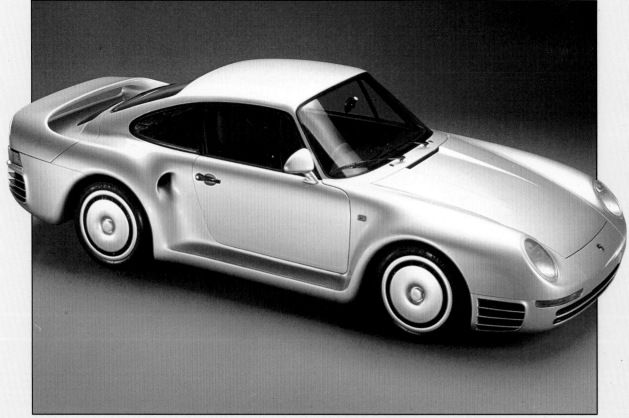

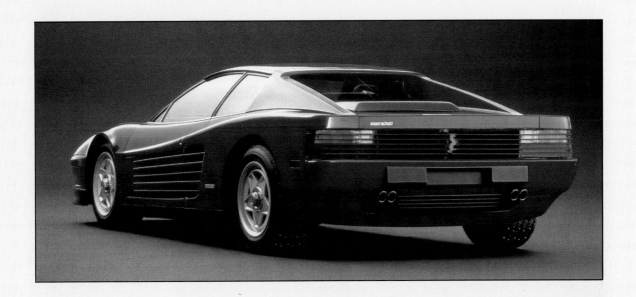

THE FASTEST ROAD CARS

The world's fastest standard production cars have always been a matter for subjective argument, as many claims have been made yet few independent tests have been conducted to verify them. As things stood in 1989, Porsche's 959 and Ferrari's F40 were probably the quickest. The Ferrari had been created to celebrate the 40th anniversary of the first car bearing the late Enzo Ferrari's name, the Porsche to continue the lengthy evolution of the original 356/911 concept. The magazine *Fast Lane* tested the F40 and the 959, and while it relied on the manufacturers' top speed claims of 201.3mph (323.8kmh) and 197mph (316.9kmh) respectively, it achieved impressive acceleration figures for the twin-turbo 2.9-litre V8 Ferrari and the twin-turbo 2.8-litre flat-six Porsche. The Italian car's 478bhp and 425lb ft of torque gave 60mph in 3.9 seconds, to 100 in 7.8 and on to 160 in 19.8! Its German rival's 450bhp, 368lb ft of torque and four-wheel drive achieved the same speeds in 4.2, 9.7 and 28.3 seconds.

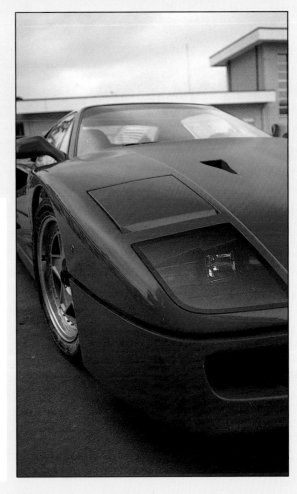

OPPOSITE *Porsche's mouthwatering 959 is the ultimate development of the 356/911 theme that has evolved over the years. Though slightly slower than the Ferrari F40, it is generally deemed the better car.*

ABOVE *Before the advent of the F40, Ferrari's Testarossa was the epitome of the road-going supercar.*

RIGHT *The F40 took over its mantle, and moved the supercar into a totally different league: the racer on the road.*

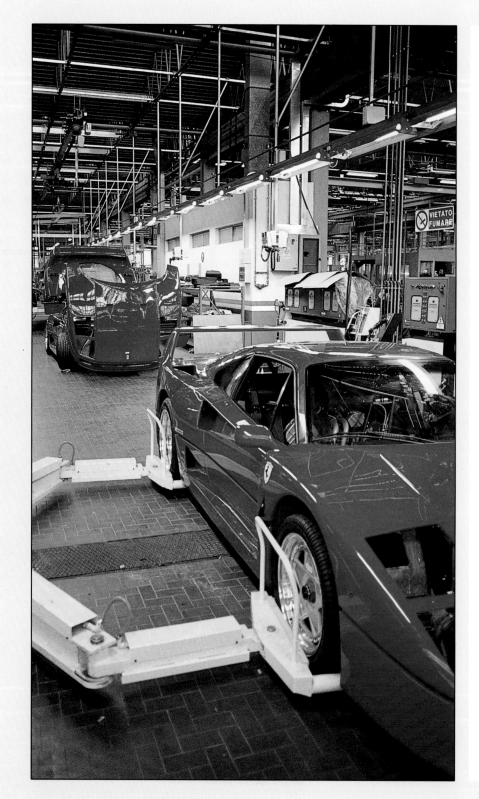

Against such figures the accepted supercars of the previous generation – the Lamborghini Countach (173mph [278kmh]), Ferrari Testarossa (181mph [291kmh]), Ferrari GTO (190mph [305kmh]) or Aston Martin Zagato (180mph [289kmh]) were left gasping. While speed limits are absurdly out of touch with the reality of modern road car technology, there are precious few places in the world where such total performance can ever be exploited.

When they were introduced in 1987, the F40 and the 959 cost £153,000 and £155,000 respectively, but the value of both limited edition machines rose dramatically once the original order books had been filled.

FAR RIGHT, ABOVE *Porsche's 961 proved that 4WD was a viable racing proposition when it competed at Le Mans in 1987.*

LEFT AND RIGHT *The F40 marked Enzo Ferrari's 40th anniversary of car manufacture. With a twin-turbo 2.9-litre V8 engine it produces 478bhp and 425 lb.ft of torque, sufficient to propel it from rest to 60 in 3.9 seconds.*

FAR RIGHT *Audi's 4WD 200 quattros won the 1988 SCCA TransAm Championship in America, where champion Hurley Haywood follows team-mate Hans Stuck.*

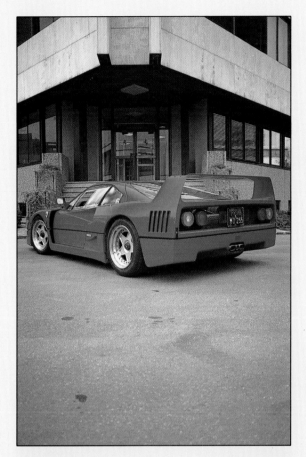

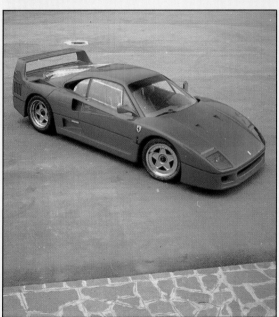

It has even acquitted itself with distinction in racing. Porsche's 4WD 961 derivative of its 959 supercar has run successfully at Le Mans, while Audi's system ran quickly and reliably in America's TransAm saloon car racing series in 1988, as did Renault's R21 Turbo in the Super Production championship. In 1989 a number of manufacturers, including Peugeot and Audi, lobbied FISA hard to permit 4WD in its future plans for the Sports-Prototype World Championship. For once, that's a case of from road to racing . . .

Anti-lock braking (standardized across a manufacturer's range for the first time by Ford in 1985 on its Granadas) is one vital road car asset that is unlikely to transfer to racing, where drivers still prefer to be the masters of their own destiny in such matters. The high cost of carbon fibre, and the need to run very high temperatures to make it function at its best, make it unlikely that carbon fibre brake discs will make the switch from racing to road.

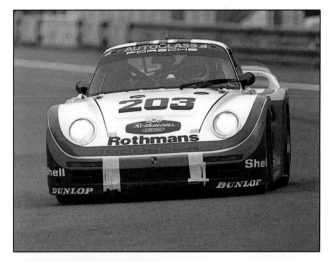

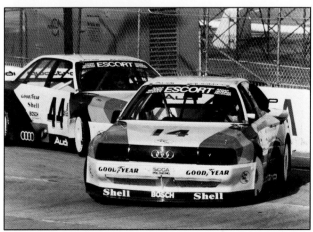

RIGHT *Ferrari's 1989 F1/89 F1 contender, designed in Britain by John Barnard, became the first clutchless Grand Prix car ever to win a race when Nigel Mansell took victory in Brazil in the first race of the season. Thereafter, however, the electronics in its electro-hydraulic semi-automatic transmission proved a constant source of unreliability in the following races.*

OPPOSITE *Porsche's PDK push-button clutchless transmission took a long time to develop in the racing 956 and 962 sportscars, but though it eventually became reliable, its success was qualified. The unit was overweight and, like the Ferrari, its racing value was questionable. However, both systems have very strong roadcar potential.*

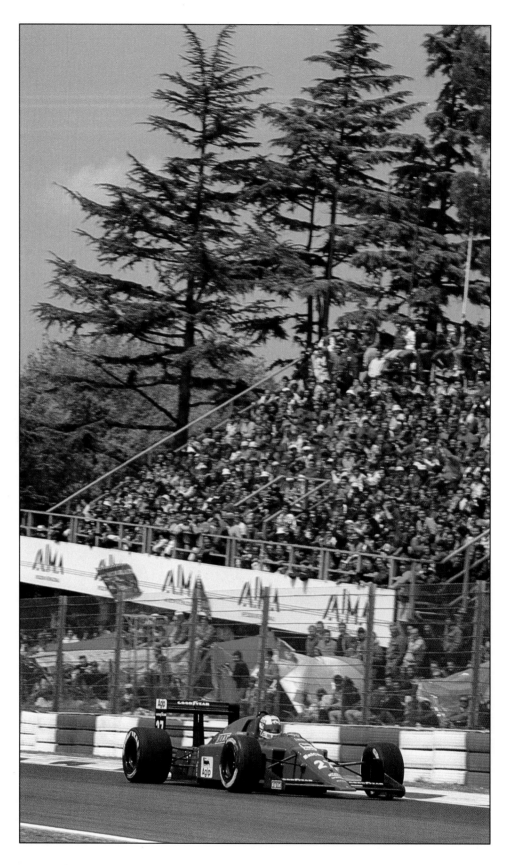

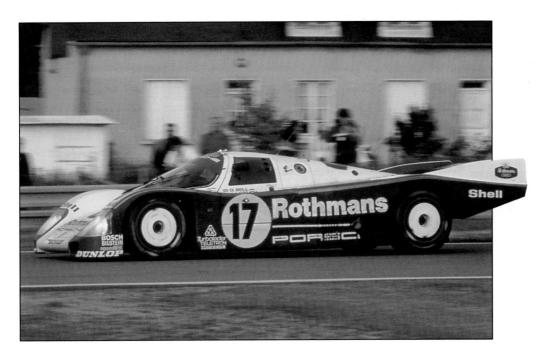

The Grand Prix world is currently at the leading edge of investigation into the use of ceramics in engines, Honda in particular having initiated intensive investigations of such materials. The technology will undoubtedly take a long time to filter down to the ordinary family car, as opposed to upmarket supercars, but when such major producers are involved – and motorsport is currently enjoying its highest level of manufacturer interest for 30 years – its eventual arrival on the street is inevitable.

More likely to benefit the everyday driver before then is the new interest in clutchless transmission. Back in the 1950s racing driver David Hobbs had success with the system devised by his father, but lack of investment hampered its development. In 1974 Lotus attempted to run an innovative automatic, electrically operated clutch on its 76s, but swapped back to conventional clutch and gearbox after encountering persistent teething problems. More recently Porsche has had qualified success in sports car racing with its push-button PDK semi-automatic system. That, however, has an inherent weight penalty.

The most successful system so far has been that devised by Briton John Barnard, who designed World Championship-winning cars for McLaren International before moving to Ferrari. Using his unique electro-hydraulic transmission, in which the driver simply changes gear by actuating pull levers mounted behind the steering wheel, Nigel Mansell swept to victory in the 1989 Brazilian GP to lead the World Championship. The potential advantages of a road car application of such a system

are presently exercising many technical minds.

Likewise, active suspension is another motor-racing seed likely to blossom in a road car application. The aim of active suspension is to insulate the chassis from road shocks, and to maintain it at a constant angle to the road. In racing this can be used to maintain the correct ride height and thus maximize ground effect; in a road car it is a means of ensuring a comfortable ride. Lotus pioneered it in racing, followed by Williams and Benetton, while GM is researching it thoroughly for road use.

Active suspension uses a computer linked to a series of sensors on each wheel. Electronic or hydraulic actuators respond incredibly fast to damp out shocks. Those who have sampled passive and active versions of the same car have no doubts about its vast potential.

There is less certainty about the concept of four-wheel steering (4WS), which has been evaluated and put into production by companies such as Mazda, Renault and Honda. The idea is that the rear wheels are interlinked with the fronts to provide a limited degree of movement. This can be a significant benefit in parking manoeuvres, but the manufacturers also claim it sharpens a car's response at speed and makes it more forgiving, and back-to-back tests have indicated that there is an advantage. The plus is nowhere near as pronounced as that of 4WD, however, and it remains to be seen how the market takes to what the sceptics see as little more than a gimmick.

THE GREATEST FIASCO

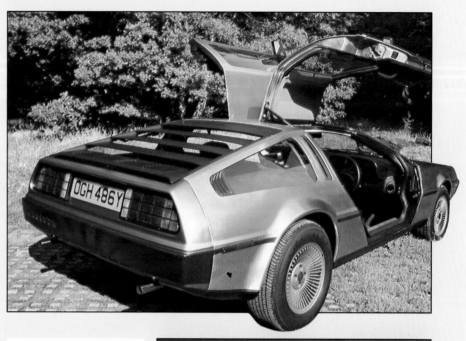

When it was announced it seemed like the answer to a region's prayers, but the De Lorean affair was to become the greatest *cause célèbre* in British motoring history, as millions of pounds of government money was poured into an ambitious project that ended in fiasco.

In March 1981 former General Motors Vice President John Z. De Lorean launched his concept of a rear-engined gull-winged sports car bearing his own name. It was not to be any ordinary car, but a volume production vehicle principally for his native North America. The bombshell was that it would be manufactured in a specially-built factory in Northern Ireland. In trouble-torn Belfast it was like manna from heaven, and De Lorean was hailed as a saviour for the 40% of the male population who couldn't find work. Initial scepticism about a car that proved rather flabby by European standards, was alleviated when Lotus became involved in its development, but 30,000 units a year for what was nevertheless a highly specialized machine with a limited market still struck seasoned observers as optimistic in the extreme.

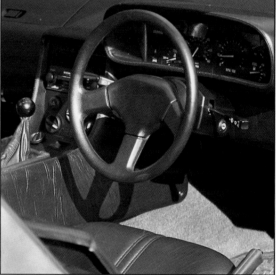

ABOVE AND RIGHT *John De Lorean's dream was to build a rear-engined two seater sports car for a mass market in the United States and Europe. The result was this sleek gullwing coupe which, through his flamboyant lifestyle and allegations of fraud and drugs dealing, was to become a cause célèbre in the motoring world.*

Then the government changed, the purse strings were pulled tighter. He continued his free-spending policies, using British taxpayers' money. Eventually the inevitable happened and funds ran out, and at that time his name became besmirched by allegations of drug offences. By the time he was acquitted the mud had stuck and the Belfast dream was over, though he never accepted that his car wouldn't one day go into production.

In his wake lay a trail of shattered local businesses, and an ongoing mystery concerning the whereabouts of at least £15m of the £80m that the British government so eagerly – and naïvely – shelled out to the silver-tongued automotive Svengali. In the words of Roy Jenkins, an MP at the time, 'Frankly, would you buy a used car company from this man?'

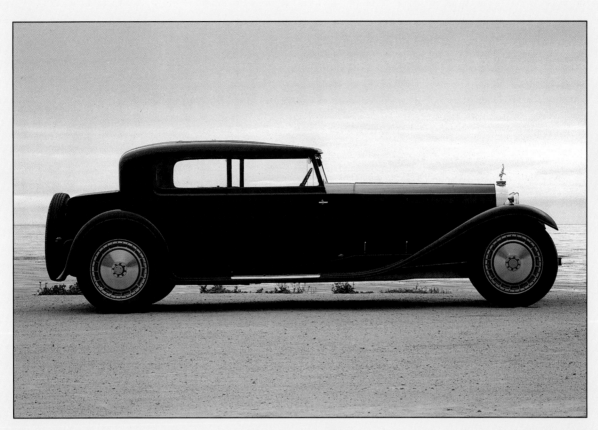

SOUND INVESTMENTS

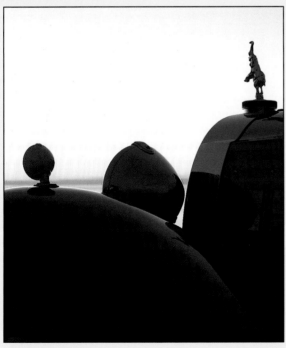

Texan oil magnate Thomas Monaghan was delighted when he paid £5.7m for one of only six Bugattis Royales ever built, yet the previous owner was even happier. Not long before he had purchased the car at auction in September 1986 for £4.6m! The fabulous Type 41 Royale limousine was Ettore Bugatti's rarest creation, and Monaghan's 1931 version was rarer still thanks to special Berline de Voyage coachwork. Just over a year later, a second Royale was sold at a Christie's auction. This 1931 model, with Kellner coachwork, was bought by Hans Thulin, a Swedish financier. His cool £5.5m purchase price remains the all-time world auction record.

ABOVE AND LEFT *Ettore Bugatti's most valuable product was the fabulous Type 41 Royale. Power came from a straight-eight engine and only six of the long wheelbase limousines were ever built, each being clothed with specialist coachwork. Today, each is worth a fortune.*

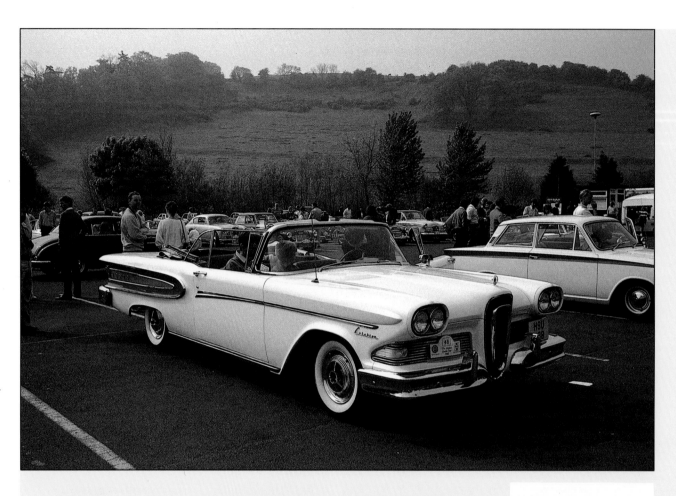

THE BIGGEST FLOP

The history of the motor industry is full of failures, but the most embarrassing flop of all time was Ford's Edsel.

It was conceived at a time when the American market was heavily into 'cars of the future', when buyers thought nothing of driving cars with fins the size of light aircraft wings and chromium decoration was at its most obtrusive. Ford's Lincoln-Mercury Division launched the Edsel on an unsuspecting public in 1958, but only after masses of market research had already boosted the budget into six figures. Part of it had gone to the poetess Marianne Moore who was paid to think up a host of attractive model names. None of them were ever used . . .

It proved a masterpiece of bad timing. By the time it was in production its arrival coincided with a hefty recession and it overlooked new trends towards less outspoken, more compact designs. Even by the standards of its day – and they were pretty low – the Edsel was a vulgar gin palace on wheels, and its appalling looks went hand in hand with its poor handling, high weight and oversize dimensions in sealing its fate.

Middle class America had been expected to buy it in its hundreds of thousands. Instead, Lincoln-Mercury only ever managed to offload 35,000 of the 5.9 or 6.7-litre monsters, and by 1960 production had ceased.

The industry couldn't work out which was more embarrassing to Ford; the fact that the ill-fated car took its name from one of Henry's sons, or that it cost the company a cool $250 million . . .

By the time the Edsel reached production, Americans were beginning to consider smaller 'compact' cars, and the new Ford was simply too garish even by the spectacular standards of the day. Middle class America, at which the car had most eagerly been aimed, voted with its feet, by going mainly to Chevrolet dealerships . . .

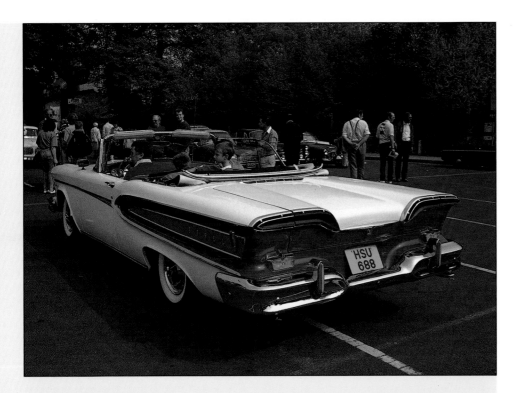

What price failure? The history of the motor industry is littered with disasters, but Ford's 1958 Edsel was a marketing blunder of unprecedented proportions in which the automotive giant totally miscalculated public tastes and requirements. The cost of that miscalculation has been estimated at $250 million . . .

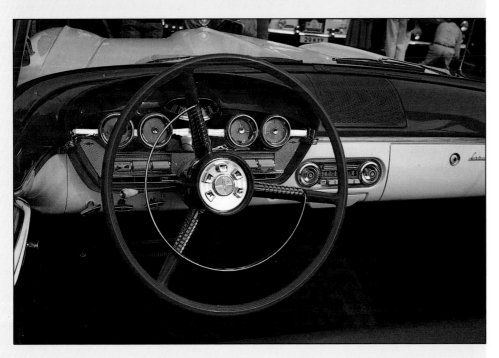

The Edsel was available in saloon and convertible guises, and with 5.9 or 6.7-litre powerplants, and Ford expected landslide sales based on the market research it had conducted. Instead, its Lincoln-Mercury division only ever sold 35,000 in its two-year production life.

LAND SPEED RECORD 1898 to 1988

YEAR	DRIVER	CAR	VENUE	SPEED mph	SPEED kmh
18.12.98	Compte Gaston de Chasseloup-Laubat	Jeantaud	Achères	39.24	62.78
17.01.99	Camille Jenatzy	La Jamais Contente	Achères	41.42	66.27
17.01.99	de Chasseloup-Laubat	Jeantaud	Achères	43.69	69.90
27.01.99	Camille Jenatzy	La Jamais Contente	Achères	49.92	79.37
04.03.99	de Chasseloup-Laubat	Jeantaud	Achères	57.60	92.16
29.04.99	Camille Jenatzy	La Jamais Contente	Achères	65.79	105.26
13.04.02	Leon Serpollet	Serpollet	Nice	75.06	120.09
05.08.02	William Vanderbilt	Mors	Ablis	76.08	121.72
05.11.02	Henri Fournier	Mors	Dourdan	76.60	122.56
17.11.02	Augières	Mors	Dourdan	77.13	123.40
17.03.03	Arthur Duray	Gobron-Brillié	Ostend	83.47	133.55
05.11.03	Arthur Duray	Gobron-Brillié	Dourdan	84.73	135.56
12.01.04	Henry Ford	Ford Arrow	Lake St Clair	91.37*	146.19*
27.01.04	William Vanderbilt	Mercedes	Daytona Beach	92.30*	147.68*
31.03.04	Louis Rigolly	Gobron-Brillié	Nice	94.78	151.64
25.05.04	Baron Pierre de Caters	Mercedes	Ostend	97.25	155.60
21.07.04	Louis Rigolly	Gobron-Brillié	Ostend	103.55	165.68
13.11.04	Paul Baras	Darracq	Ostend	104.52	167.23
25.01.05	Arthur MacDonald	Napier	Daytona Beach	104.65*	167.44
30.12.05	Victor Héméry	Darracq	Arles-Salon	109.65	175.44
23.01.06	Fred Marriott	Stanley Rocket	Daytona Beach	121.57	194.51
08.11.09	Victor Héméry	Benz	Brooklands	125.95	201.52
16.03.10	Barney Oldfield	Benz	Daytona Beach	131.27*	210.03*
23.04.11	Bob Burman	Benz	Daytona Beach	141.37*	226.19*
24.06.14	L. G. Hornsted	Benz	Brooklands	124.10	198.56
17.02.19	Ralph de Palma	Packard	Daytona Beach	149.87*	239.79*
27.04.20	Tommy Milton	Duesenberg	Daytona Beach	156.03*	249.64*
17.05.22	Kenelm Lee Guinness	Sunbeam	Brooklands	133.75	214.00
06.07.24	René Thomas	Delage	Arpajon	143.31	229.29
12.07.24	Ernest Eldridge	Fiat	Arpajon	146.01	233.61£
25.09.24	Malcolm Campbell	Sunbeam	Pendine Sands	146.16	233.85
21.07.25	Malcolm Campbell	Sunbeam	Pendine Sands	150.76	241.21
16.03.26	Henry Segrave	Sunbeam	Southport Sands	152.33	243.72

YEAR	DRIVER	CAR	VENUE	SPEED mph	SPEED kmh
27.04.26	John Godfrey Parry Thomas	Babs	Pendine Sands	169.30	270.88
28.04.26	John Godfrey Parry Thomas	Babs	Pendine Sands	171.02	273.63
04.02.27	Malcolm Campbell	Bluebird	Pendine Sands	174.88	279.80
29.03.27	Henry Segrave	Sunbeam	Daytona Beach	203.79	326.06
19.04.28	Malcolm Campbell	Bluebird	Daytona Beach	206.95	331.12
22.04.28	Ray Keech	White Triplex	Daytona Beach	207.55	332.08
11.03.29	Henry Segrave	Golden Arrow	Daytona Beach	231.44	370.30
05.02.31	Malcolm Campbell	Bluebird	Daytona Beach	246.09	393.74
24.02.32	Sir Malcolm Campbell	Bluebird	Daytona Beach	253.97	406.35
22.02.33	Sir Malcolm Campbell	Bluebird	Daytona Beach	272.46	435.93
07.03.35	Sir Malcolm Campbell	Bluebird	Daytona Beach	276.82	442.91
03.09.35	Sir Malcolm Campbell	Bluebird	Bonneville Salt Flats	301.13	480.20
19.11.37	George Eyston	Thunderbolt	Bonneville Salt Flats	312.00	499.20
27.08.38	George Eyston	Thunderbolt	Bonneville Salt Flats	345.50	552.00
15.09.38	John Cobb	Railton	Bonneville Salt Flats	350.20	560.32
16.09.38	George Eyston	Thunderbolt	Bonneville Salt Flats	357.50	572.00
23.08.39	John Cobb	Railton	Bonneville Salt Flats	369.70	591.52
16.09.47	John Cobb	Railton Mobil Special	Bonneville Salt Flats	394.20	630.72
05.08.63	Craig Breedlove	Spirit of America	Bonneville Salt Flats	407.45*	651.92*
17.07.64	Donald Campbell	Bluebird	Lake Eyre	403.10	644.96
02.10.64	Tom Green	Wingfoot Express	Bonneville Salt Flats	413.20	661.12
05.10.64	Art Arfons	Green Monster	Bonneville Salt Flats	434.02	694.43
13.10.64	Craig Breedlove	Spirit of America	Bonneville Salt Flats	468.72	749.95
15.10.64	Craig Breedlove	Spirit of America	Bonneville Salt Flats	526.28	842.04
27.10.64	Art Arfons	Green Monster	Bonneville Salt Flats	536.71	858.73
02.11.65	Craig Breedlove	Spirit of America – Sonic 1	Bonneville Salt Flats	555.48	888.76
07.11.65	Art Arfons	Green Monster	Bonneville Salt Flats	576.55	922.48
13.11.65	Bob Summers	Goldenrod	Bonneville Salt Flats	409.27**	654.83**
15.11.65	Craig Breedlove	Spirit of America – Sonic 1	Bonneville Salt Flats	600.60	960.96
23.10.70	Gary Gabelich	The Blue Flame	Bonneville Salt Flats	622.41	995.85
04.10.83	Richard Noble	Thrust 2	Black Rock Desert	633.47	1013.47

*Not recognized by European authority **Wheeldriven record
NOTE: Up to 1963, all contenders listed were driven through their wheels. After that, only Campbell and Summers used wheeldriven cars. All others were pure thrust projectiles.

The most controversial of all Land Speed Record projects was undoubtedly the Budweiser Rocket. From the start, project mentor Hal Needham, a Hollywood stuntman, decided to go against the regulations calling for two runs within an hour through a timed kilometre or mile. Instead, the tricycle rocket car was timed through a measured 52.8 ft at Edwards Air Force Base in California's Mojave Desert in December 1979. The timing equipment was not officially recognized either, and comprised radar scanners which originally gave intrepid pilot Stan Barrett's speed as 30mph after a fuel tanker had driven across the base. Needham eventually claimed 739.666mph, and that his car had broken the Sound Barrier. Others noted that many previous contenders could have claimed much higher records for themselves had they taken their peak, not average, speeds, and remained thoroughly sceptical about the whole thing. The 'record' remains unofficial.

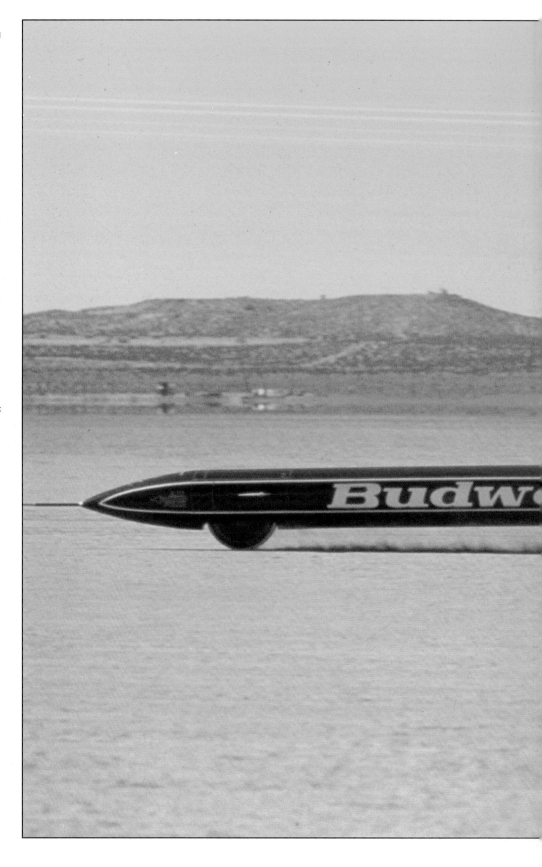

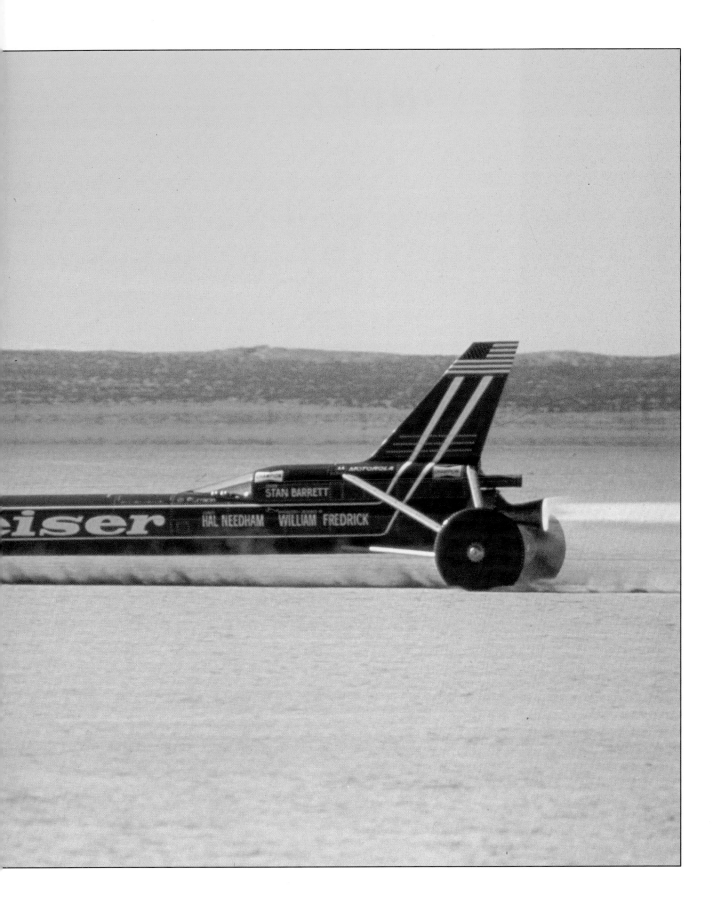

INDEX

Page references in *italic*
refer to captions.

PICTURE CREDITS

Richard Noble, Project Thrust pp 8-39, 62b, 122; Popperfoto pp 40 (main picture), 57; Goodyear pp 40 (inset), 50, 54, 55; Daimler-Benz pp 42, 43a; National Motor Museum, Beaulieu pp 43b, 46, 61b; Indianapolis Motor Speedway pp 44, 45, 70, 71, 72, 73, 74, 76, 100; J Baker Collection pp 47, 67, 104, 106, 107, 113, 114, 115l, 118; Donnington Collection/J Baker pp 79a, 82, 83b, 85; Chas K Bowers and Sons Ltd pp 48, 49, 60, 61a; Jaguar Cars p 51; Quarto Publishing p 52, 63, 124; Firestone pp 56, Author pp 58, 62a, 102b; L.A.T. Photographic Library pp 64, 66, 68, 75, 77, 78, 79b, 80, 81, 83a, 84, 87, 89, 90, 91, 92, 93, 94, 96, 97, 98, 101b, 102a, 103, 110, 115r, 116; Renault Archives pp 99, 101a; Peugeot pp 108, 109; Lancia p 111; Porsche pp 112, 117; Christie's Auction House p 119; Andrew Morland pp 120, 121.